JOHN BROOKES
GARDEN
DESIGN
WORKBOOK

DORLING KINDERSLEY
LONDON · NEW YORK · STUTTGART

A DORLING KINDERSLEY BOOK

First American Edition, 1994
2 4 6 8 10 9 7 5 3 1

Published in the United States by
Dorling Kindersley Publishing, Inc., 95 Madison Avenue,
New York, New York 10016

Published in Great Britain by Dorling Kindersley Limited.
Distributed by Houghton Mifflin Company, Boston.

ISBN 1 56458 559 X

Reproduced in Italy by Typongraph
Printed and bound in Italy by Graphicom

CONTENTS

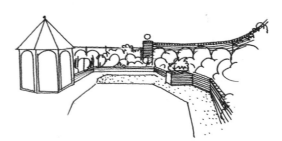

INTRODUCTION

To many people, the very idea of a designed garden is alien. It is perceived as an unnecessary exercise, appropriate only to the gardens of stately homes. The reality is quite different – in fact, the smaller the area, the more it needs a layout to maximize its potential. Plants are seen too often as the *raison d'être* of a garden, and of course they are

Organic shapes
The shapes of plant masses are critical in expressing the harmony and proportion of a garden design.

Design and planting
The combination of design forms in a garden and the textural overlay created by plant material never cease to intrigue me.

an essential part of it, filling in the pattern, but a designed layout takes into account the function of the space: its paths, changes of level, places to sit, access points, and storage facilities. A garden designer must assess these functions in relation to the house to create a unified garden layout.

It is an odd fact (and any designer will substantiate this) that to design for oneself is far more difficult than to design for someone else; often there are many personal associations with the existing garden to be overcome. The newcomer to garden design may well be doubly confounded – he or she may have all the inhibiting associations, but none of the practical techniques needed to overcome them.

Design details
A good garden design will show sympathetic patterning even down to the details of paving.

The object of my *Garden Design Workbook* is to explain the design process to everyone interested in evolving a garden plan. I will lead you through the design maze step by step, explaining the process as I use it in my own garden design practice and as I teach it at my school.

Before getting to the specifics of garden design, however, and before your eye is trained to discern what is right and what is wrong in terms of shapes, you need to

Natural impact
Bold plants impose their own pattern on a design.

be able to look, see, and enjoy the shapes that are all around us in our daily lives. The practical information in the *Garden Design Workbook* will help you to do this, but you will also have to help yourself by learning to express yourself on paper. Take your pens and paper, abandon inhibitions, and prepare to experiment. Do not be afraid to try out fresh ideas: draw graphic shapes, make bold patterns, and use color freely.

Geometric shapes
Experiments with bold, abstract shapes can lead to strong patterns for a garden design.

Bold, linear shapes are only one source of pattern. Naturally occurring patterns are all around us in the veins of leaves, in bark, in landscapes of hills and fields. Learn to see patterns in everything around you, from paving stones to fabrics. Once you get your eye accustomed to recognizing pattern, you will realize that little is random or haphazard. Pattern may be determined by weather, the forces of nature, by man in farming, by machines, and so on. The seemingly random undulation of a landscape seldom occurs without reason, and so kicking a length of hose about in the hope of

Textile patterns
Pattern is everywhere. You can draw inspiration from the graphic patterns of textiles.

The patterns of landscape
Geology, topsoil, flora, and climate create natural patterning, modified by the ways we use the land.

The patterns of detail
Close inspection of detail can be inspirational – for example, in dry-stone walls or cracked earth.

getting inspiration for a "naturalistic" garden pattern will not necessarily be successful. Pattern, and hence design, has a strength and a logic which, I suspect, is why the strong geometry of a formal garden is so attractive to many people.

Geometry, balance, and symmetry are qualities we associate with classical orders in architecture and that are to be found in great Renaissance gardens. But from the beginning of the twentieth century we have had another option – that of asymmetry – which can be just as ordered. Abstract, asymmetrical patterns fit far better into the proportions of the average contemporary garden, and give the designer greater flexibility to fulfil the demands of a brief, than rigid classical, formal patterns. Of course, there are, and will always be, situations for which the formal approach remains eminently suitable, and individual elements of classical design can always be used in your garden layout; experiment with moving different shapes about, possibly overlapping them, to create an abstract composition.

Once you have learned to be confident with your pens, pencils, tracing paper overlays, and cutouts, you can experiment with design options, entirely in the abstract at first. When you have mastered these skills, I will show you how to relate shapes to the proportions of a house using a basic module or grid.

You then need to relate your pattern to the requirements of a real site. Begin to decide what should go where and why – terracing in sun or shade, a path to the shed or garage, places for herbs, to store logs, to hide the compost.

Once you have come to terms with two-dimensional pattern, I will teach you to start thinking in terms of three-dimensional blocks. These blocks will represent different levels of the garden, where appropriate, or different heights of plant material. At this stage, you are still not quite thinking about actual planting; rather you are considering balance and proportion. For ultimately, a garden should be a pleasant place to be in, sheltered from the world between the masses of planting, or looking out over a fine open view.

A garden design is a three-dimensional project (four-dimensional if you add time and therefore plant growth). I will show you how to move from the two-dimensional plan to the three-dimensional projection. The design concepts of symmetry, asymmetry, abstraction,

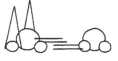

Symmetry

Asymmetry

Counterpoise

The designer's choices
Just as objects can be arranged to make a pleasing composition on a mantelpiece, so the elements of a garden can be moved around to create a successful design.

Two dimensions
A garden pattern is a collage of shapes – areas of grass, water, paving, and planting – that should combine to be visually exciting while functioning on a practical level.

Three dimensions
When heights of structures and plants are added, a two-dimensional scheme takes on three-dimensional reality.

proportion, dimension, and scale may be confusing at first, but in a real design these concepts come to life. Think of the garden designer as a painter putting oil on canvas to represent a scene or a person, or simply to delight the eye by use of color and texture. Visit an art gallery and examine twentieth-century abstract paintings as well as studying the old masters. The work is endless in its variety, but you will see how every painter has sought new ways to present us with a very rich library of visual experience – upon which the designer can call. Sculptors too may inspire your garden designs and because they work three-dimensionally, you might feel that their work has even more relevance to the activity of the garden designer, who is also working in these three dimensions.

Learning from artists
Ben Nicolson (1894-1982) used collage to contrive extraordinarily stimulating shapes that repay close study by garden designers.

Garden design should not be confused with the craft of gardening. Gardening involves realizing your plan for the site through planting and construction. By thinking too soon about installation and the practical realities of soil and plant material, you will kill the spontaneity of the design process (though eventually, of course, it has to be tempered by all sorts of factors, including financial considerations). But the first stage of garden design, which I wish to share with you in my *Garden Design Workbook*, should be free of all these inhibitions, enabling you to be liberal and ambitious with your ideas.

The power of pattern
Asymmetry and geometry are combined within a formal framework in this Bauhaus poster of 1923.

It is a daunting thought that there are no two identical gardens in the world, for there are no two identical sites. Moreover, because your design vision is exclusive to yourself, your garden design will be a unique creation.

John Brookes

PROPORTION

PROPORTION IN DESIGN means visual balance. In garden design terms it is the art of making a garden sit well within its site, and then of making plant masses, water features, lawns, and terraces cohere in a balanced (or proportioned) relationship. A garden looks right only when all its elements are in proportion to each other.

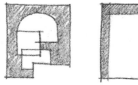

THE IMPORTANCE OF PROPORTION

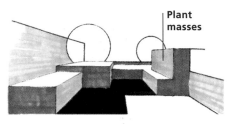

Well-balanced elements

Disproportionate shapes

These illustrations show how shapes in proportion (far left) make a more pleasing design than an unbalanced selection of shapes (left).

USING PROPORTIONAL SHAPES

Correct proportioning is as vital in designing the ground plan as it is in planning heights.

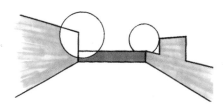

Plant masses

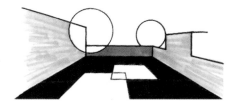

THE GARDEN SPACE
A standard rectangular garden, with fencing and two trees to consider.

GROUND PATTERN SHAPES
The shapes of the ground pattern relate to the scale of the site.

THREE-DIMENSIONAL SHAPES
The plant masses work because they are in proportion to the ground pattern.

THE POWER OF PROPORTION
Simple geometric shapes combine in this garden to create a well-proportioned design.

Angled paving slabs juxtapose effectively with the pool

The bold circular pool works successfully in this site because it is balanced in scale by the graveled area surrounding it

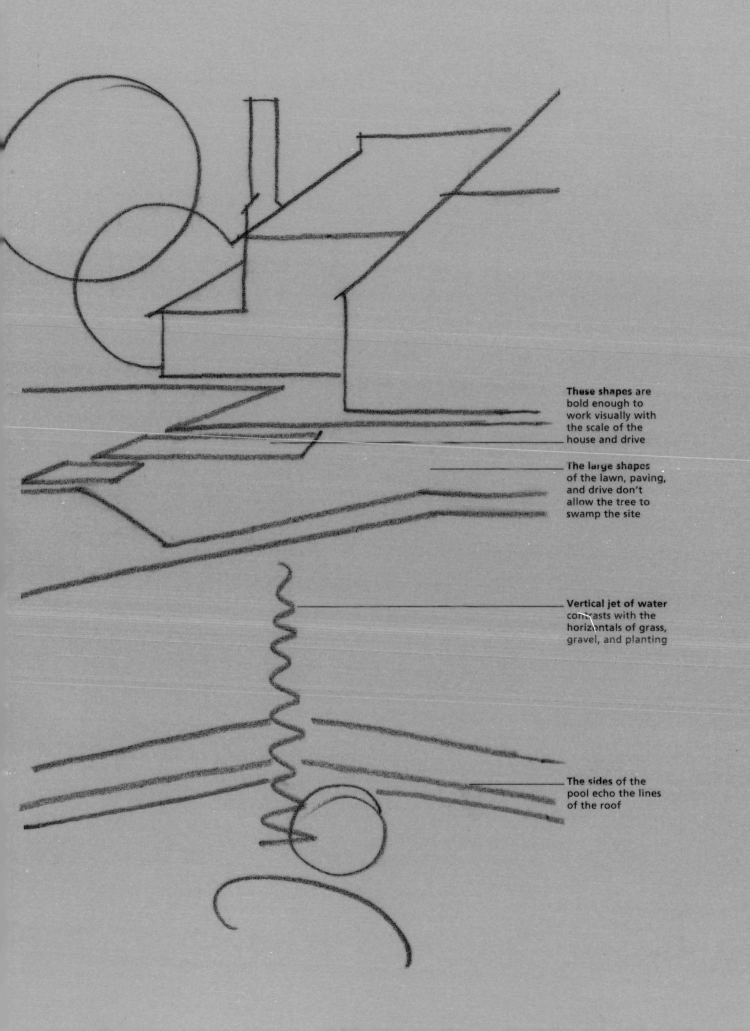

These shapes are bold enough to work visually with the scale of the house and drive

The large shapes of the lawn, paving, and drive don't allow the tree to swamp the site

Vertical jet of water contrasts with the horizontals of grass, gravel, and planting

The sides of the pool echo the lines of the roof

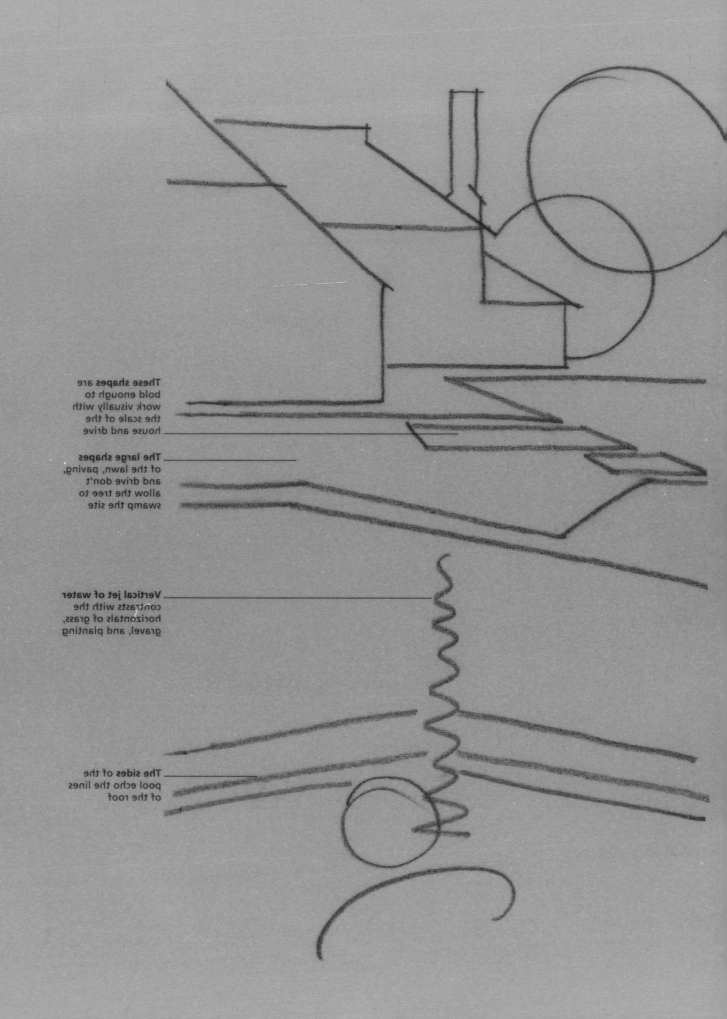

A BALANCED DESIGN
The simplicity of this modern garden design melds the proportions of the house and its surrounding planting to the entrance drive and neighboring tree.

PATTERN

ALL GARDEN DESIGNS begin with pattern. In theory, these patterns can take any form you like. In practice, they have to take into account limitations such as awkward corners which are difficult to construct or plants which need a certain width of bed. There will also be aesthetic constraints. To work well, a pattern must be in proportion to the house, the site, and its boundaries (see pages 8 and 16). Some believe symmetry to be the essence of a successful pattern, but asymmetry can be just as classic and is less of a straightjacket.

ESTABLISHING A PATTERN

Whether a pattern is symmetrical or not, the shapes within it should always be in proportion.

Guiding grid
(see pp.16-17)

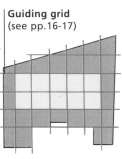 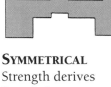 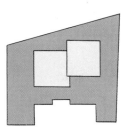 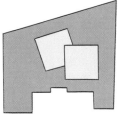 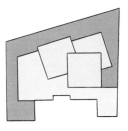

FORMAL PATTERN
This overcomes the site's disproportion.

SYMMETRICAL
Strength derives from balance.

ASYMMETRICAL
This pattern begins to add interest.

ABSTRACT
Moved, the shapes look more subtle.

PRACTICAL
Adding shapes creates a basic plan.

A GEOMETRIC SOLUTION
The simple abstract geometry of wood pads on water leads the eye onward.

THE CLASSICAL APPROACH
Classic simplicity provides the design answer in one view, although it lacks subtlety.

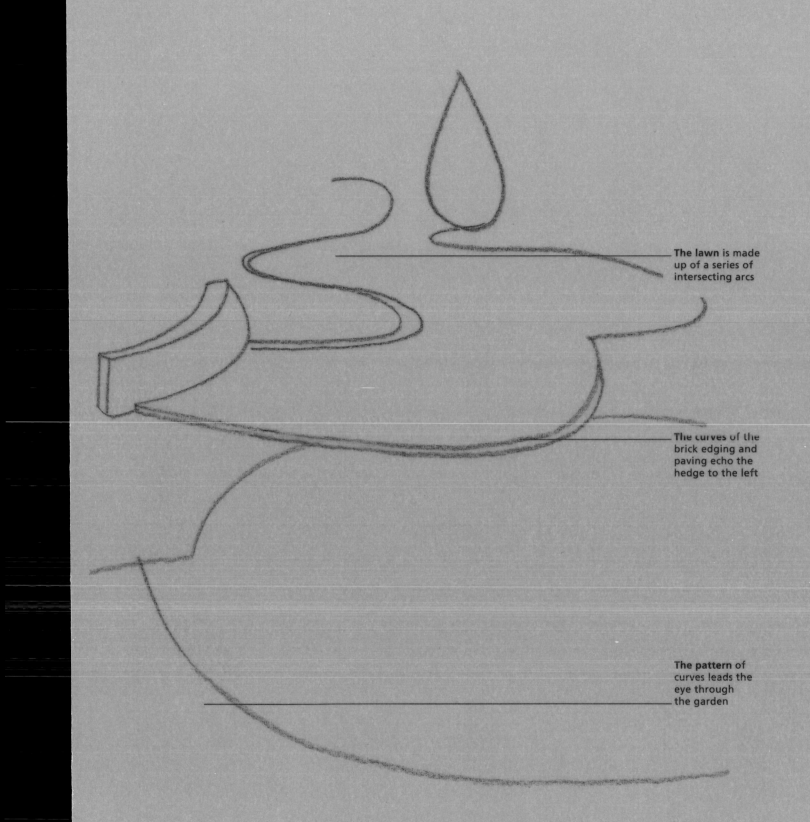

The lawn is made up of a series of intersecting arcs

The curves of the brick edging and paving echo the hedge to the left

The pattern of curves leads the eye through the garden

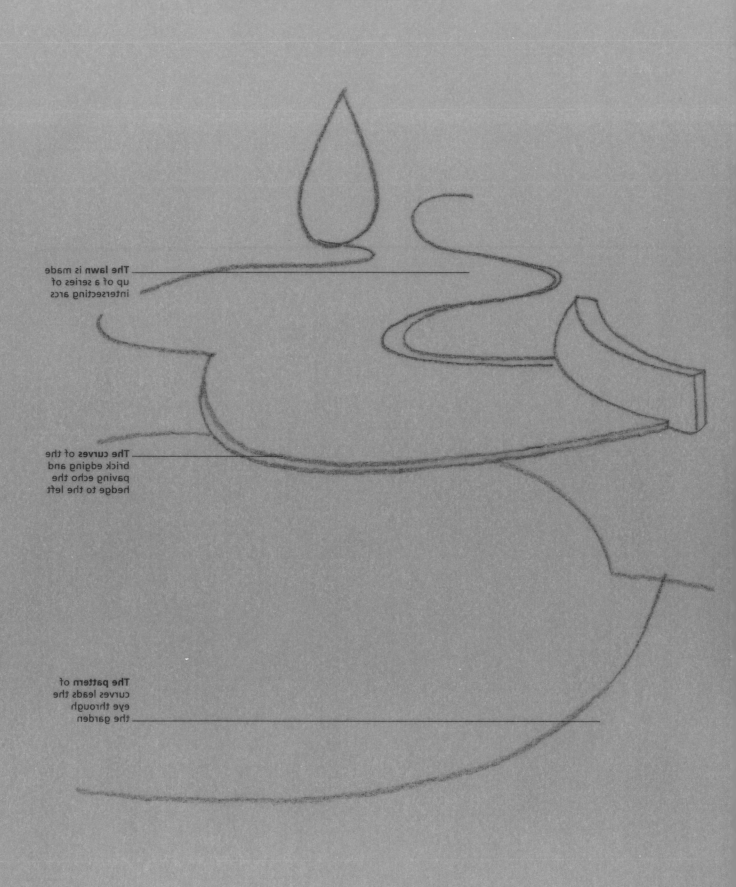

STYLING WITH CURVES
Strong patterns do not have to be angular. Geometric curves
derived from circles and arcs read more strongly within the
shape of a rectangular garden than free-flowing shapes.

MASSES & VOIDS

A WELL-DESIGNED GARDEN is a balance of masses (plants and structures) and voids (the open areas between them). To create harmony between them, you first need to evolve a pattern that is pleasing in itself, then to see if it works in terms of masses and voids.

SIMPLE RELATIONSHIPS

This is a starter exercise to teach you to see patterns as masses and voids.

DESIGN TIPS

◆ Put aside the drawbacks of your own garden for a moment. Think of it as just an empty space that you can fill with any shapes you choose.

◆ The first stage of design has nothing to do with horticulture and everything to do with making space work in a visually satisfying way.

MAKING THE BASIC SHAPES

Cut out a piece of paper to represent the shape of your garden. Its proportions should be broadly correct, but it does not need to be drawn to scale at this stage.
Then cut out a variety of paper shapes and experiment with them on the paper. The paper shapes you use will be dictated by your sense of style; the way you arrange them will derive from what feels right to you. Remember: you are making patterns and thinking about shapes, not planning your own garden yet.

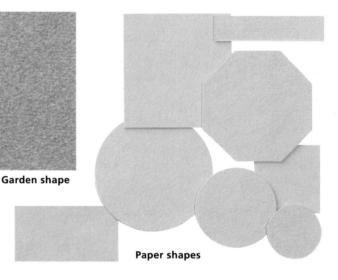

Garden shape

Paper shapes

GOOD PATTERN, POOR DESIGN
This pattern is harmonious, but does not work as masses and voids – there is no space (void) adjacent to the house.

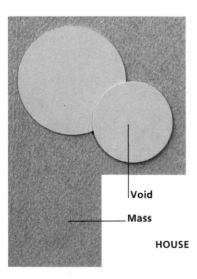

Void

Mass

HOUSE

A BETTER USE OF SPACE
A bolder approach, this pattern uses more of the plot's area, but creates some uncomfortable angles.

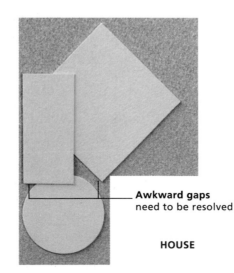

Awkward gaps
need to be resolved

HOUSE

A POWERFUL SOLUTION
A strong design: the overlap between the octagon shapes makes a focal point to be developed.

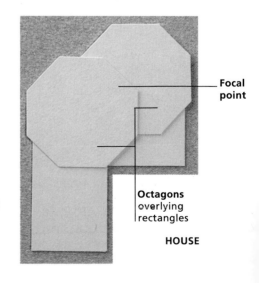

Focal point

Octagons overlying rectangles

HOUSE

TRANSLATING PATTERNS INTO MASSES AND VOIDS

The simplest patterns, translated into masses and voids, can yield graphic results.

SIMPLE GEOMETRY
The initial plan for this splendidly formal garden is no more than three concentric squares.

AN EXPERIMENT WITH CIRCLES
Three circles are all that make up this pattern in which the two large circles provide balance and the smaller one movement. The challenge is to make them work as masses and voids.

When it is projected (far right), the two circles are linked to make one space. The design emerges as a fluent sequence of curves, making excellent use of the available space.

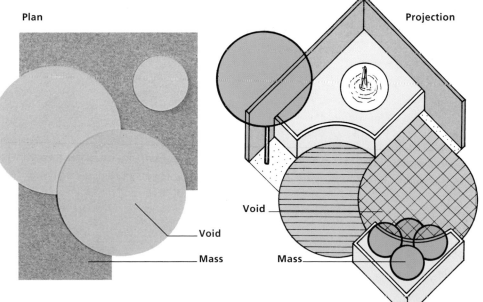

Plan

Void

Mass

Projection

Void

Mass

WHY USE A GRID?

THE FACADES OF MOST HOUSES are designed with proportion in mind. The architect plans the structure on units or modules of space which may reflect the scale of the rooms. If the garden designer can plan the garden using the same module as the architect – or a proportion of it, perhaps half or double – the house and garden will fit well together visually.

FINDING A RHYTHM

Even the flat facade of a house will have a rhythm of windows and doors that you can analyse.

SIMPLE DIVISIONS
The large sliding window on the left is the dominant feature of this facade. See how the rest of the house can be divided using the same module.

Sliding window

Divisions do not have to align exactly with the house

Bay

A HIDDEN MODULE
The bay dominates the facade of this house, but its width is not repeated as a whole unit. Halve the bay's width, however, and you discover the rhythm of the construction on which to base a grid.

A STRICT PATTERN
This asymmetrical house is designed to a strict proportion based on the width of the bay. Halving this module gives a workable grid for the garden.

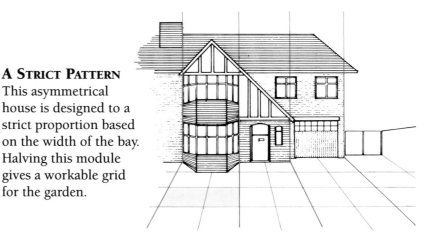

TURNING THE GRID
This elegant facade could have a module of four or five squares. By turning the resulting grid at 45°, the attached building is tied into the overall plan and the proportion is retained.

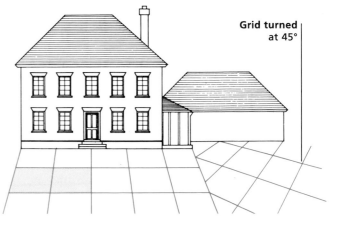

Grid turned at 45°

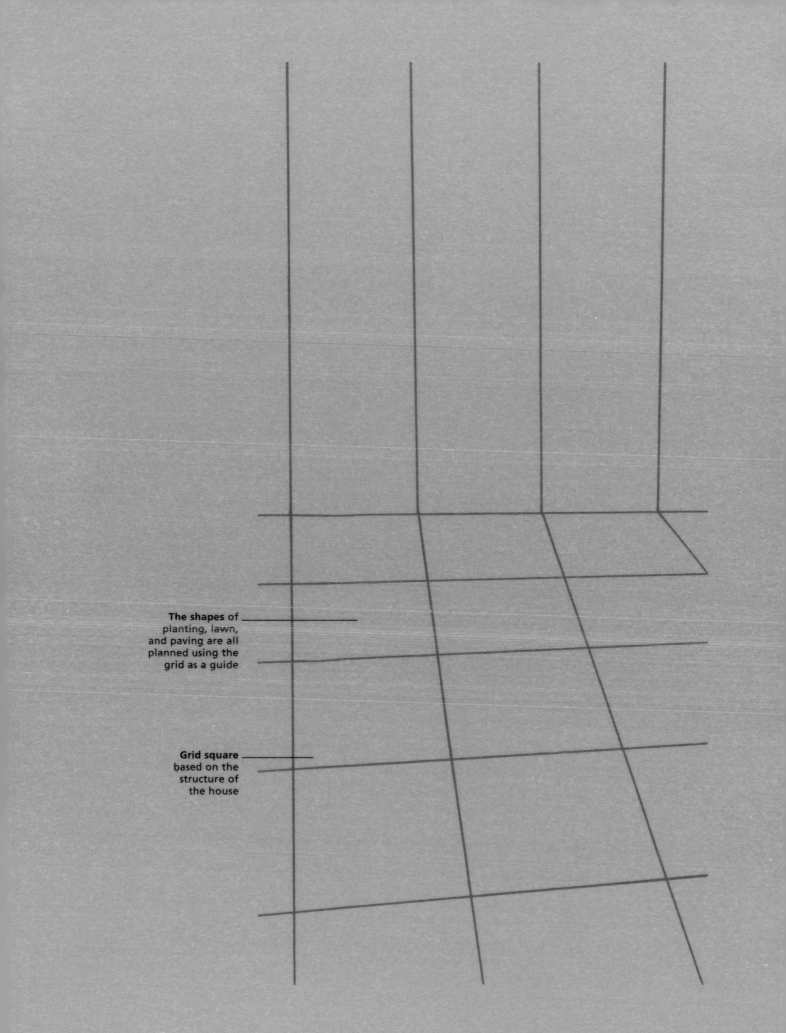

The shapes of planting, lawn, and paving are all planned using the grid as a guide

Grid square based on the structure of the house

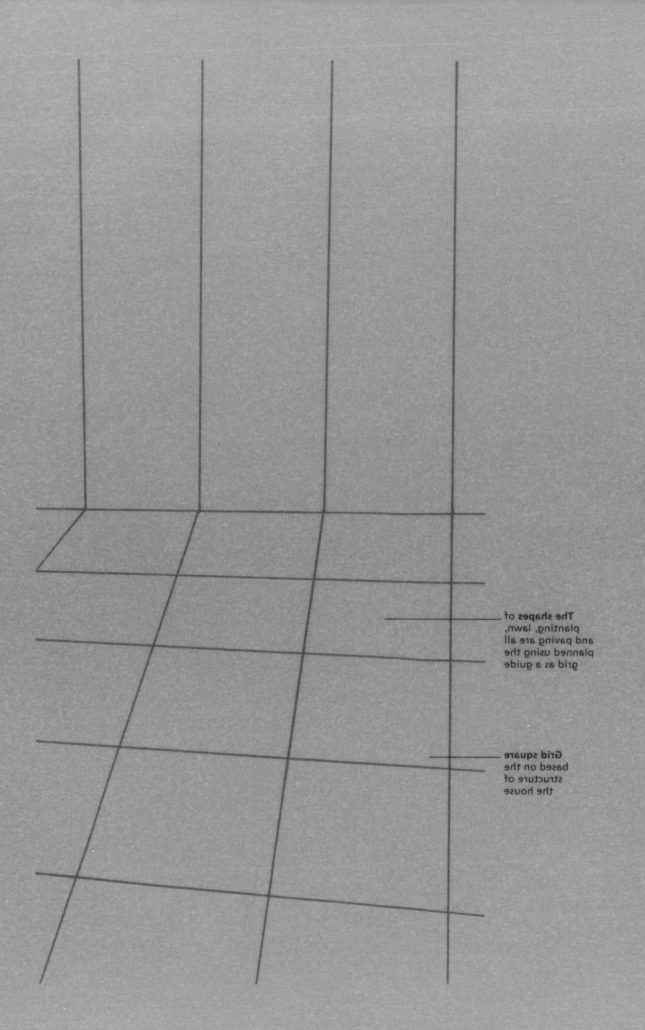

ENLARGING THE GRID

Increasing the size of the grid square – doubling or quadrupling it as you approach the far boundaries of the garden – ensures that the ensuing pattern will relate to larger elements outside the site.

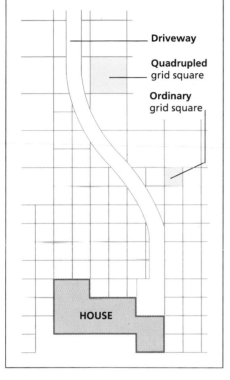

Driveway

Quadrupled
grid square

Ordinary
grid square

HOUSE

THE GRID IN ACTION

In this "live" example, the lines on the tracing paper overlay demonstrate how the basic grid square has been based on the rhythm of windows and door on the house. The same grid is then extended over the garden.

FROM GRID TO GARDEN

THE OWNERS OF THE STYLISH PERIOD HOUSE shown on page 15 wanted their garden to be divided into three units: a hard-surfaced, contained area near the house where the dog could be left safely outside when the owners were out, a middle "garden" area, and a paved terrace at the end, overlooking the river. The garden is long and narrow, and already has a built-up terrace at the river end. The rhythm of the house is easy to establish: there are three units, expressed as door, window, and window on the ground floor, and also as three windows on the floor above. This gives a grid module which is one third of the width of the house.

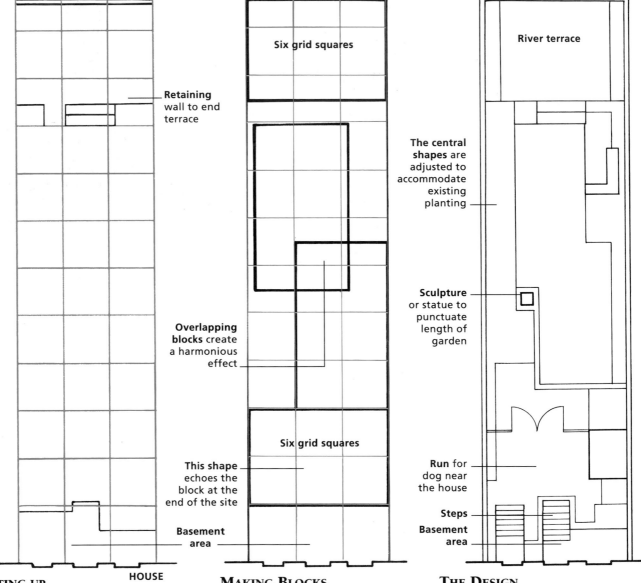

Retaining wall to end terrace

Six grid squares

River terrace

The central shapes are adjusted to accommodate existing planting

Overlapping blocks create a harmonious effect

Sculpture or statue to punctuate length of garden

Six grid squares

This shape echoes the block at the end of the site

Run for dog near the house

Basement area

Steps
Basement area

HOUSE

SETTING UP
The plan is turned so that the designer can work as if looking into the site from the house. Then the grid is drawn ready for use. The horizontal lines of the grid are drawn starting from the basement.

MAKING BLOCKS
Multiples of the grid squares can be experimented with. These are the building blocks and can be used to make patterns. The grid itself can now be abandoned: the blocks contain the correct proportions.

THE DESIGN
The rigid geometry of the building blocks has been modified to accommodate existing planting, but the design remains essentially true to the proportions of the blocks, and so to the proportions of the house.

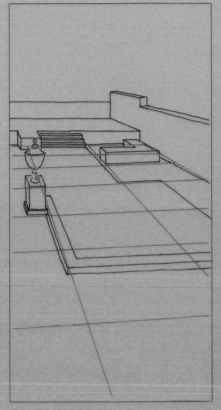

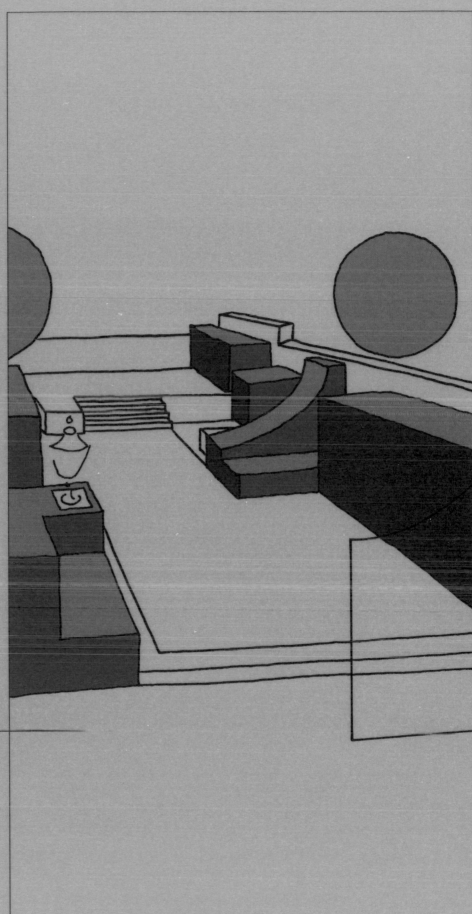

The areas near the
house remain
uncluttered by
planting, balancing
the bold masses
of plants in the
area beyond

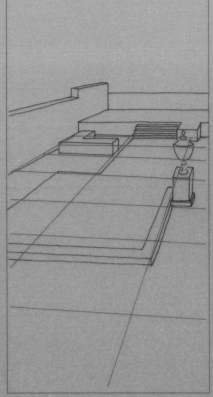

The areas near the house remain uncluttered by planting, balancing the bold masses of plants in the area beyond

THE GRID AND THE GARDEN

The grid has been laid over the garden and it is now possible to see how the ground pattern was determined. The structural essentials, including the steps, back wall, and raised terrace, have been drawn in so that their relationship to the grid can also be assessed.

THE THIRD DIMENSION

The scale and shape of plant masses give the central part of the site unity, yet link visually with the terraces. The shapes of the plant masses, as conceived in bold blocks, are shown on the tracing paper overlay.

EQUIPMENT & DRAFTING SKILLS

GARDEN DESIGN IDEAS will be accurate on site only if they are planned with precision from the outset. With practice, patience, and care, anyone can produce competent working garden drawings, but some simple, inexpensive equipment is needed.

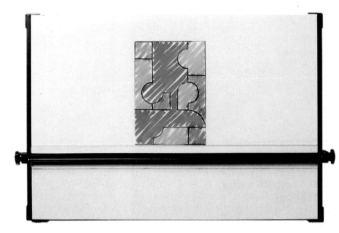

ESSENTIAL EQUIPMENT

The equipment you need to draw garden plans is all standard and readily available from art shops.

THE DRAWING BOARD
Drawing boards should be at least 3ft (1m) wide, and the angle should be adjustable. Some models have useful parallel motion rulers attached.

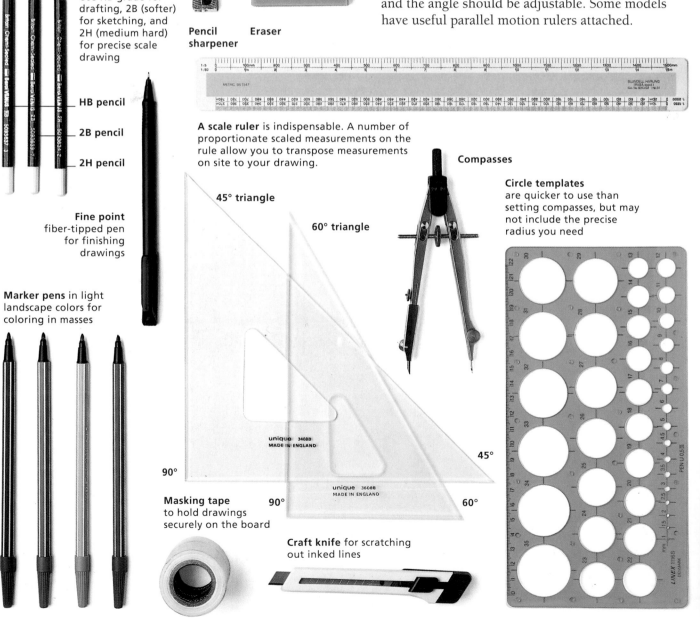

Pencils
Use HB grade for drafting, 2B (softer) for sketching, and 2H (medium hard) for precise scale drawing

Pencil sharpener

Eraser

HB pencil

2B pencil

2H pencil

Fine point fiber-tipped pen for finishing drawings

A scale ruler is indispensable. A number of proportionate scaled measurements on the rule allow you to transpose measurements on site to your drawing.

Compasses

Circle templates are quicker to use than setting compasses, but may not include the precise radius you need

45° triangle

60° triangle

45°

90°

60°

90°

Marker pens in light landscape colors for coloring in masses

Masking tape to hold drawings securely on the board

Craft knife for scratching out inked lines

BASIC DRAFTING SKILLS

Accurate drawing abilities and a sharp pencil are the prerequisites for drafting working plans.

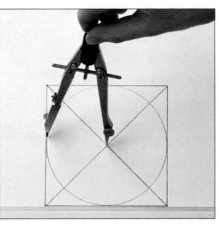

DRAWING SQUARES

Draw a horizontal line and measure it. With a 45° triangle, draw vertical lines of the same length from either end. Join them. Draw two diagonals with the triangle to link the diagonally opposite corners.

DRAWING CIRCLES

Draw a square as shown, left. The intersection of the diagonals marks its center. Put the compass point on the intersection, spread the compasses to reach the nearest part of the square, and draw a circle.

SUBDIVIDING SQUARES

Draw a square as shown, far left. Draw a vertical line and a horizontal line through the center. Draw diagonal lines in the four smaller squares you have made to find their centers and draw a circle in each.

TYPES OF PAPER

Through all the stages of a developing garden plan, use tracing paper – it allows you to make overlays and see through the different layers. If your drawing board is other than white, put white cardboard behind the paper. Use the lightest-weight tracing paper for your early workings and a heavier weight, preferably 90 gram, for the final drawing.

DESIGNING WITH SHAPES

When you can draw the basic shapes described above, use them as units to compile complex forms. Experiment by turning your tracings and setting them at various angles. Create further possibilities by overlaying more tracings in different colors.

HOW TO MEASURE

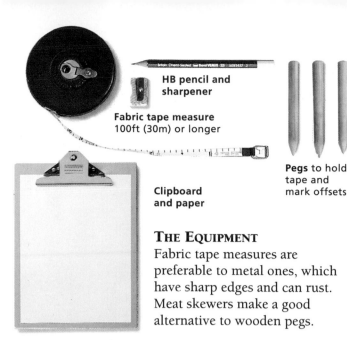

HB pencil and sharpener

Fabric tape measure
100ft (30m) or longer

Clipboard and paper

Pegs to hold tape and mark offsets

ACCURATE MEASUREMENT of the site is the essential first stage in designing a new garden. It is not difficult, though it does require care. Draw the outline of your garden freehand on a clipboard pad, then record all the measurements you make of the site on this rough plan, following the advice given here. You will then be ready to make a scaled drawing that will be the starting point for any subsequent design.

THE EQUIPMENT
Fabric tape measures are preferable to metal ones, which have sharp edges and can rust. Meat skewers make a good alternative to wooden pegs.

THE FIRST STAGES

First measure the house, noting the positions of doors and windows.

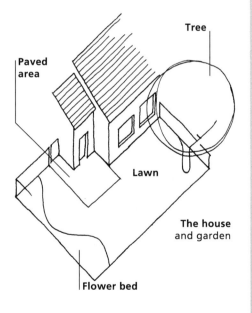

Tree

Paved area

Lawn

The house and garden

Flower bed

ROUGH PLAN OF THE SITE
To make a rough plan, go into the garden with the equipment shown above. You will need to measure all boundaries, the house (including doors and windows), flower beds, and so on. Use a peg to hold one end of the tape. To position fixed features such as trees and utility covers, you need to take offsets (see facing page). Record your detailed measurements as on the plan shown.

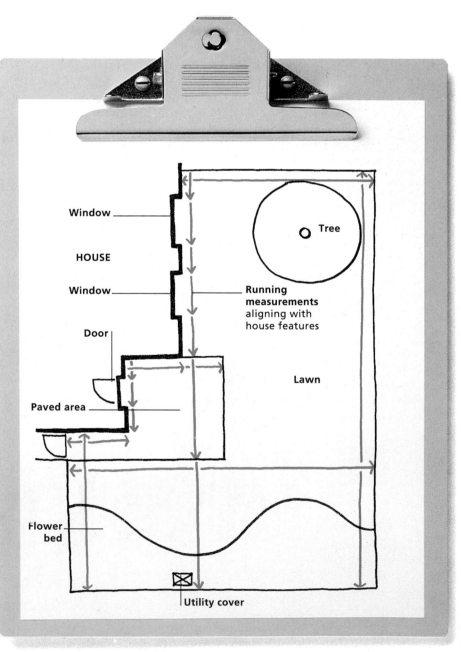

Window

HOUSE

Window

Door

Paved area

Flower bed

Tree

Running measurements aligning with house features

Lawn

Utility cover

MAKING A WORKING SKETCH

As you take each measurement, record it on the rough plan on your clipboard. Virtually all houses have 90° corners and most boundaries lead away from the house at right angles, but even when things look square, measure to check.

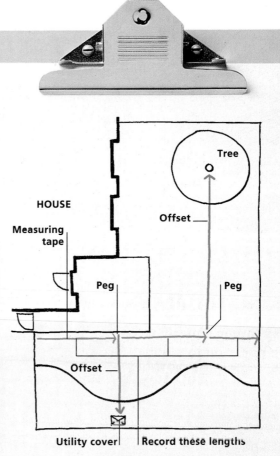

HOUSE
Measuring tape
Peg
Tree
Offset
Peg
Offset
Utility cover | Record these lengths

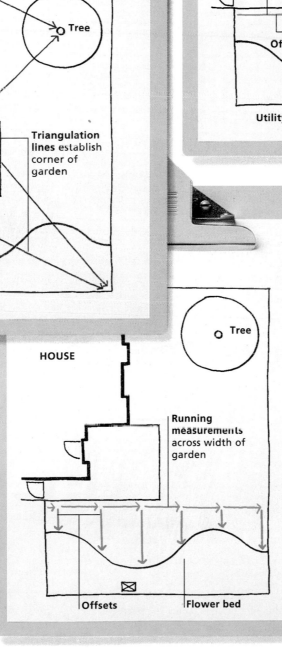

Triangulation lines establish position of tree

HOUSE

Tree

Triangulation lines establish corner of garden

HOUSE

Tree

Running measurements across width of garden

Offsets | Flower bed

TRIANGULATING
To record the exact position of a fixed object such as a corner of the garden or a tree, measure it from two points on the house.

RECORDING OFFSETS
To establish positions of features such as trees and utility covers while measuring, note the exact position of your tape while it is laid across the garden. Place pegs beside the tape opposite features whose positions you wish to determine. Measure from the start of the tape to each peg. Then measure the distances from the pegs to the features. These measurements are known as offsets. Their accuracy can be checked by triangulating (see opposite).

DEFINING CURVES
Take 90° offsets (as above) at regular intervals – say every 3ft (1m) – to record the general shape of curves such as in a flower bed or lawn. Mark each measurement and join the points freehand.

DRAWING TO SCALE

ONCE THE SITE HAS BEEN MEASURED and you have entered the dimensions on the rough plan, it is time to make a scale drawing of the plot. Choose a scale that will allow you to get the entire drawing on one piece of tracing paper that will fit on your drawing board. Use a sharp 2H pencil: it is important to be as accurate as possible. You can thicken up certain lines later (see facing page).

MAKING THE PLAN

Start by taping a piece of tracing paper on to your drawing board.

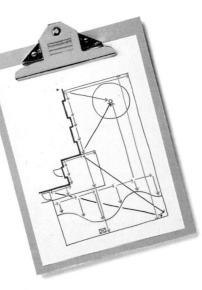

The raw material for your scale drawing is your freehand rough plan with all dimensions recorded (see page 20).

EQUIPMENT NEEDED

Drawing board ◆ tape ◆ tracing paper ◆ triangle(s) ◆ scale or ordinary ruler ◆ 2H pencil ◆ sharpener ◆ compass ◆ eraser ◆ pen to finish drawing

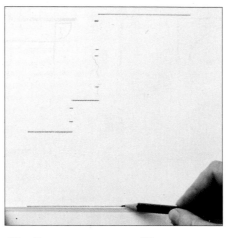

1 START WITH THE HOUSE
Rule a horizontal line, then draw to scale the shape of the back/front/sides of the house, as appropriate. Mark positions of windows, doors, bays, and recesses.

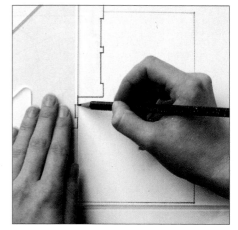

2 DEVELOP THE OUTLINES
Draw right angles where they occur and establish the outlines of the plot and garden buildings. Measure lines to scale. Join positions to fill in house detail.

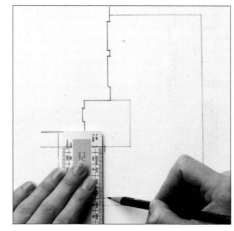

3 TRANSFERRING OFFSETS
Mark on the plan where you had placed your tape. Record the peg points, then measure off at 90° to position the features.

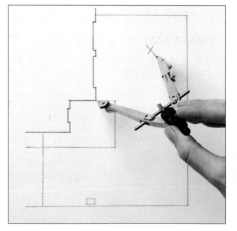

4 TRIANGULATED POINTS
Set the compass to the scaled measurement. Work from the point of triangulation and draw arcs. The feature lies where they intersect.

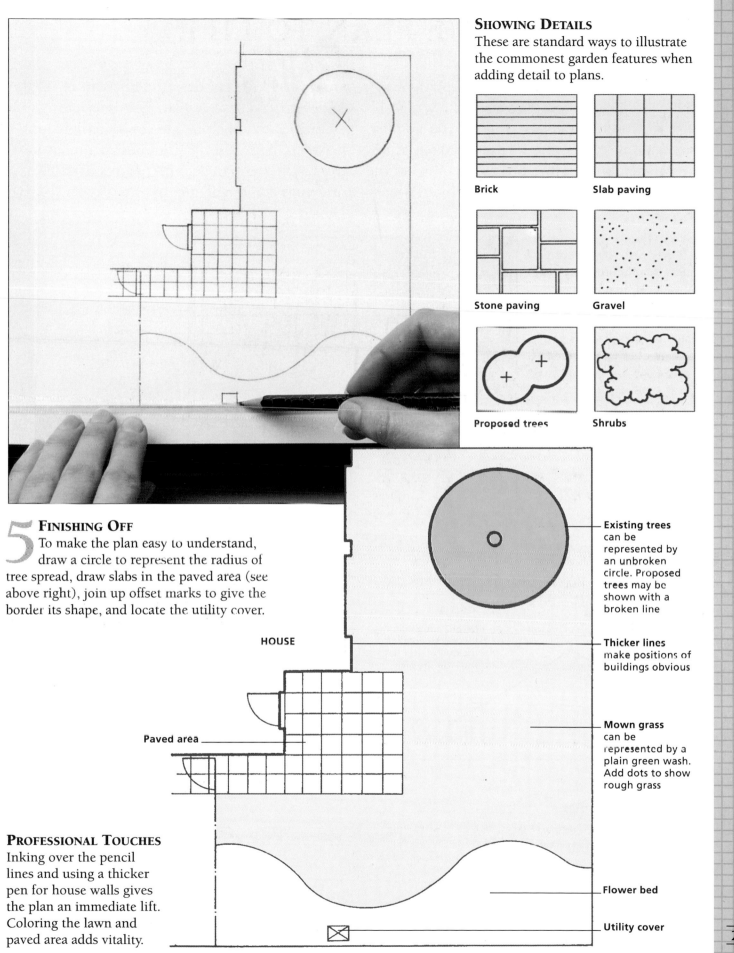

BRINGING THE PLAN TO LIFE

A WELL-FINISHED SCALE PLAN is essential, but there are times when it does not show clearly all you would like to see. It gives you no idea, for example, of heights of proposed structures or plants and therefore little sense of what the garden will look like to someone in it. There are several kinds of drawing that can be used to develop your scale plan. Sections and elevations establish heights and relationships between them; a projection does a similar job from a different angle; and perspective drawings add a realistic quality.

SCALE PLAN
All the proposed structures and main plantings on the site appear on a finished plan, but this gives you no idea of their heights. To establish these factors you need to draw an elevation (below) or a projection (facing page).

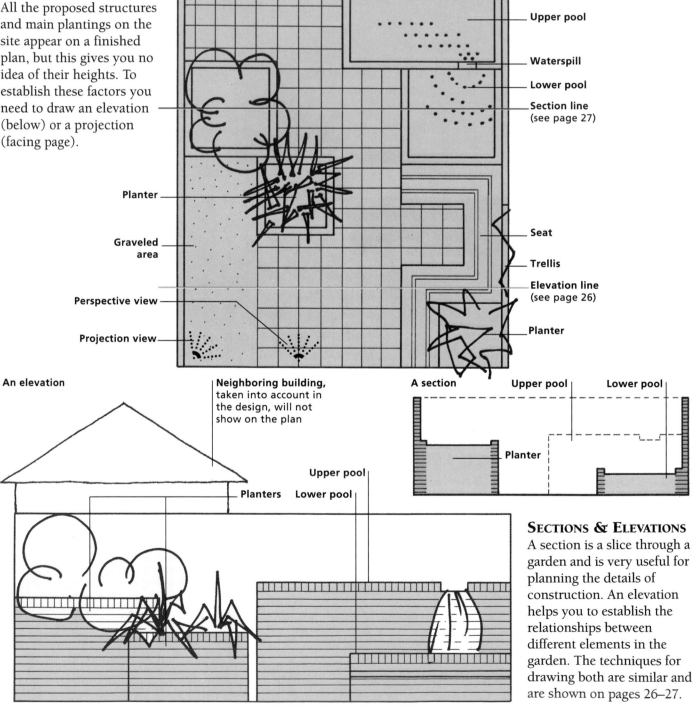

Upper pool

Waterspill

Lower pool

Section line
(see page 27)

Planter

Graveled area

Seat

Trellis

Elevation line
(see page 26)

Perspective view

Projection view

Planter

An elevation

Neighboring building, taken into account in the design, will not show on the plan

Planters   Lower pool

Upper pool

A section   Upper pool   Lower pool

Planter

Upper pool

SECTIONS & ELEVATIONS
A section is a slice through a garden and is very useful for planning the details of construction. An elevation helps you to establish the relationships between different elements in the garden. The techniques for drawing both are similar and are shown on pages 26–27.

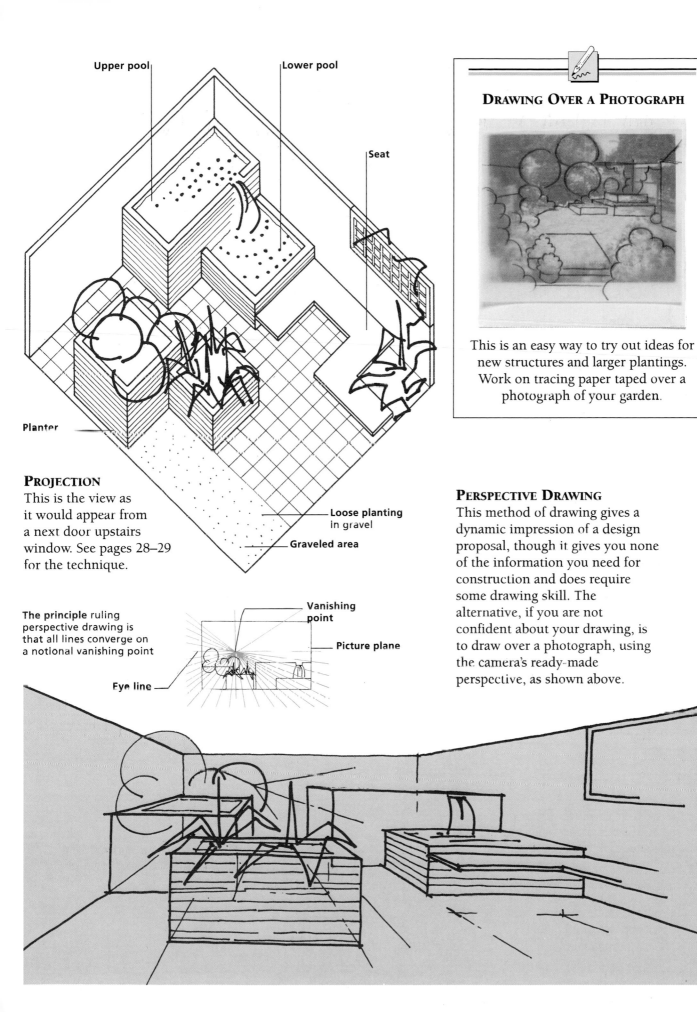

Upper pool

Lower pool

Seat

Planter

PROJECTION

This is the view as it would appear from a next door upstairs window. See pages 28–29 for the technique.

The principle ruling perspective drawing is that all lines converge on a notional vanishing point

Vanishing point

Picture plane

Eye line

Loose planting
In gravel

Graveled area

DRAWING OVER A PHOTOGRAPH

This is an easy way to try out ideas for new structures and larger plantings. Work on tracing paper taped over a photograph of your garden.

PERSPECTIVE DRAWING

This method of drawing gives a dynamic impression of a design proposal, though it gives you none of the information you need for construction and does require some drawing skill. The alternative, if you are not confident about your drawing, is to draw over a photograph, using the camera's ready-made perspective, as shown above.

ELEVATIONS & SECTIONS

AN ELEVATION GIVES A UNIQUE VIEW of the way plant masses and structures in a plan will interrelate. Planning and plotting the height of each element gives a preview of the finished garden from ground level. A section is a slice through a garden made using similar techniques.

EQUIPMENT NEEDED

Drawing board ◆ scale ruler or ordinary ruler ◆ tracing paper ◆ tape ◆ large triangle ◆ pencil ◆ sharpener ◆ eraser ◆ fiber-tipped pen to finish the drawings

MAKING AN ELEVATION

Tape your scale plan on the drawing board and place tracing paper over it. Now decide how much of the garden you wish to show in your elevation.

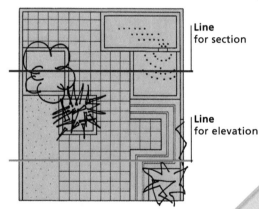

Line for section

Line for elevation

CHOOSING A LINE

The green line is where the elevation will be taken from. Only features above it will appear in the drawing. The red line will be used to develop a section (see facing page).

1 MAKE THE FIRST LINES
Draw a horizontal line clear of the top of the plan. This is the base line of your elevation. Draw in the heights of any existing walls or structures which may affect your final design. Then, working up from the elevation (green) line, draw vertical lines up through the intersections of the lines on the plan. These vertical lines should extend above the base line: lengthen or shorten them as you decide on the heights of new structures.

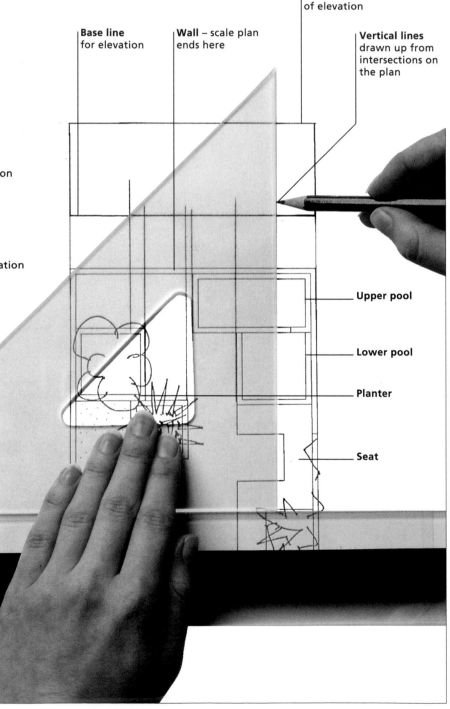

Back wall of elevation

Base line for elevation

Wall – scale plan ends here

Vertical lines drawn up from intersections on the plan

Upper pool

Lower pool

Planter

Seat

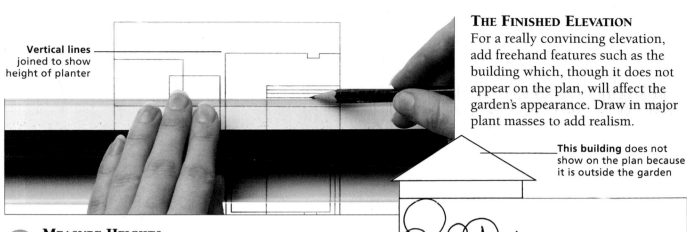

Vertical lines joined to show height of planter

THE FINISHED ELEVATION

For a really convincing elevation, add freehand features such as the building which, though it does not appear on the plan, will affect the garden's appearance. Draw in major plant masses to add realism.

This building does not show on the plan because it is outside the garden

2 MEASURE HEIGHTS

Working to scale, decide and measure off the heights of the different structures, then join the verticals. For a professional result, copy your elevation onto plain paper, ink over it, and add details in pen.

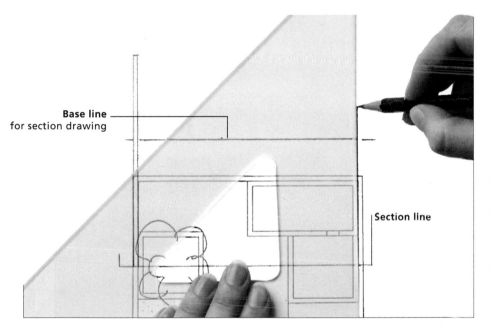

Base line for section drawing

Section line

TAKING A SECTION

Sections (or cross-sections) are slices through a design. Their main use is to clarify details prior to construction.

1 DRAW A SECTION LINE

Select the part of the garden through which you wish to take a cross-section and draw a line across it – in this case, the red line on the plan (see facing page). This is the section line. Draw in a base line above the plan. Draw vertical lines up from the section line just as you would when making an elevation.

2 ESTABLISH HEIGHTS

Decide on and mark heights of structures on the verticals. Join these marks with horizontals.

THE FINISHED SECTION

By revealing the proposed heights of structures, a section can serve as a design check before building.

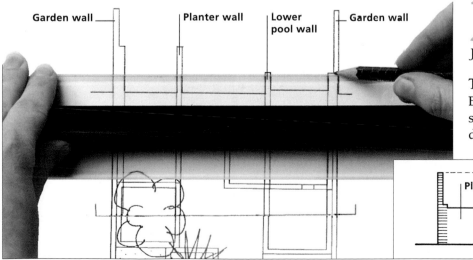

Garden wall | Planter wall | Lower pool wall | Garden wall

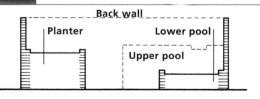

Back wall

Planter | Lower pool

Upper pool

PROJECTING A PLAN

THE VALUE OF DRAWING A PROJECTION is that it enables you to visualize in three dimensions (length, breadth, and height) what you have designed on a plan. A projection works only when you have structures – plants are difficult to draw from this aerial angle. What you achieve is the view from next door's upstairs window. Remember to draw heights to the same scale as ground dimensions.

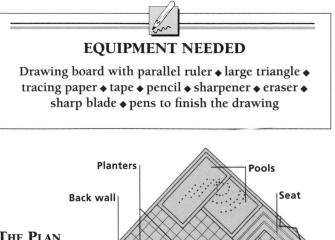

Planters

Back wall

Pools

Seat

Gravel

THE PLAN
This shows a proposal for adding planters, a seat, and linked pools to a garden. If you find it hard to visualize the built result, follow steps 1 to 6 to draw a projection.

DRAWING A PROJECTION

A projection is like a pop-up plan and will make your garden plan come alive.

1 POSITION THE PLAN
Use a triangle to position the plan at a 45° angle to the parallel ruler on your board. Tape down.

2 OVERLAY TRACING PAPER
Put your tracing paper at right angles to the ruler and tape it down. Using a triangle, trace the outline of your plan in pencil.

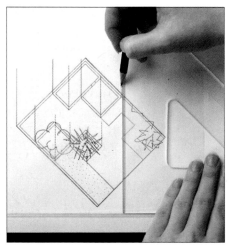

3 DRAW UP VERTICALS
Using a triangle to keep your lines at 90° to the ruler, draw vertical lines up from each point of intersection on the plan.

4 MARK OFF HEIGHTS
Measure and mark the different heights, working to the same scale as the plan. Then join up the points you have projected.

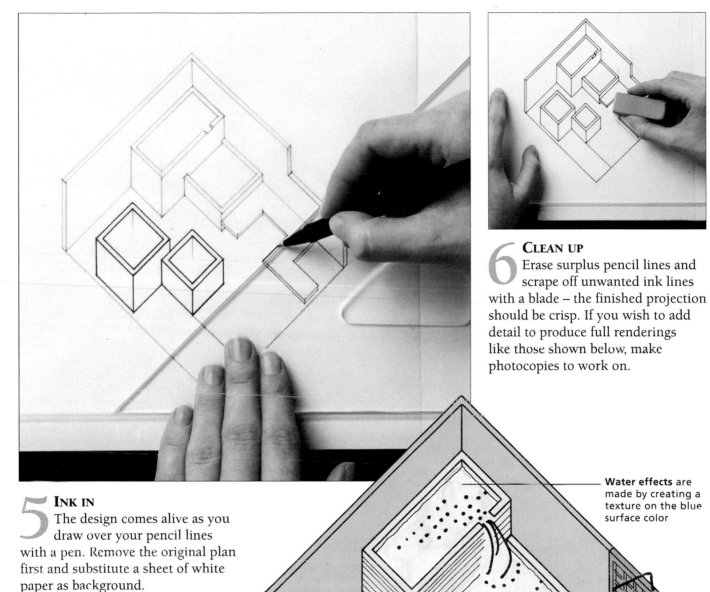

5 INK IN

The design comes alive as you draw over your pencil lines with a pen. Remove the original plan first and substitute a sheet of white paper as background.

6 CLEAN UP

Erase surplus pencil lines and scrape off unwanted ink lines with a blade – the finished projection should be crisp. If you wish to add detail to produce full renderings like those shown below, make photocopies to work on.

PROJECTING A CYLINDRICAL SHAPE

Draw a circle. Mark points on it. Decide on the height of the shape, measure up from each point and make another set of marks. Join these to create an identical circle.

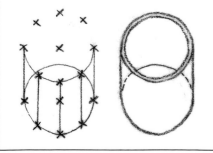

A COLORED PROJECTION

A projection looks more realistic if details such as plant shapes and paving are inked in and colored.

Water effects are made by creating a texture on the blue surface color

Planting is indicated by simple colored shapes

Dots represent a graveled area

29

CASE STUDY: A COUNTRY GARDEN

TWO ADJOINING COTTAGES in a village had been combined into one house, and the new owners wanted the gardens to be replanned. The rear of the "new" house has a sunny exposure and looks uphill toward an old cherry orchard. From the top of the site there is a wonderful view down over the house. An unsightly road runs beside the garden and this will need to be screened.

BEFORE THE SURVEY

I walked around the site to get an idea of its possibilities.

THE BUILDING STYLE
The house (shown right) is built of mellow stone in a traditional cottage style.

THE GARDEN AS I FOUND IT
This is the main part of the garden, with the road running alongside. The house is off to the right.

Neighboring house

Road

Orchard

House

Lane

THE LOCATION
The village is a farming community with most houses backing on to open country.

QUESTIONNAIRE

Before you begin to plan a garden there are some basic questions you should ask yourself (or the owner). The questions that follow are those I asked the owners of the garden I am about to replan.

Q Are you avid gardeners? Do you have any preferences about features and types of plant?

A *We like to garden, but it is not our only leisure activity and we are not plant specialists. We would, however, like you to plan a pool and a rose bed.*

Q To remake a site this large is a sizeable task. The design must be completed in one go, but would you prefer to implement it in stages?

A *It makes sense to us to reshape the garden in phases, with the court-yard at the rear of the house being remade first.*

Q Do you have any specific requirements which I should bear in mind while designing your garden?

A *No, not particularly. What we would like is a garden that is suitable for most purposes – and especially for outdoor entertaining.*

LOOKING FOR POSSIBILITIES

I established where the best views are and found the most agreeable places to make seating areas.

THE INITIAL SKETCH

My first sketch records the main features of the site that I will not be able to alter.

PRACTICAL TIPS

◆ On your first rough plan record sunny, shady, and windy areas.
◆ Note neighboring buildings, trees, and features that are seen from the garden.
◆ Note soil type(s) and local materials.

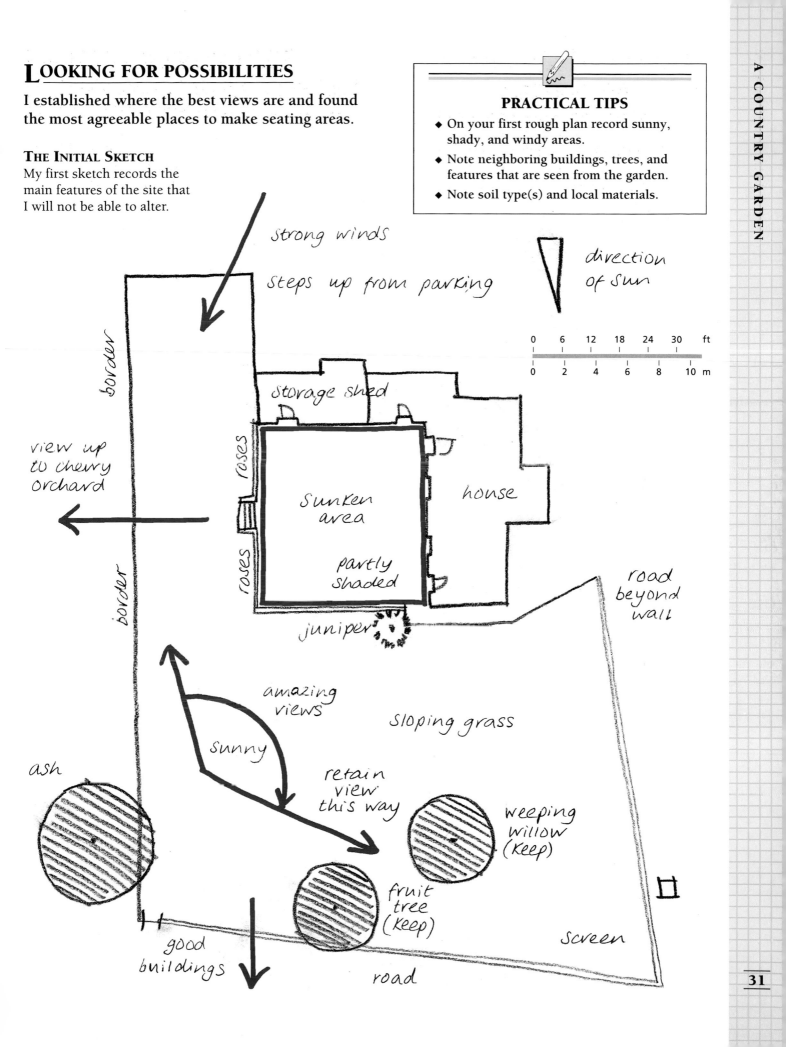

strong winds

steps up from parking

direction of sun

0 6 12 18 24 30 ft

0 2 4 6 8 10 m

border

storage shed

view up to cherry orchard

roses

roses

sunken area

partly shaded

house

road beyond wall

border

juniper

amazing views

sloping grass

sunny

retain view this way

ash

good buildings

fruit tree (keep)

weeping willow (keep)

road

screen

SITE SURVEY

MAKE A DETAILED SURVEY at the outset. You will need it very soon and there is no better discipline to make you look closely at every aspect of the site. Make enlarged drawings of individual areas if you cannot fit detailed dimensions on your main plan.

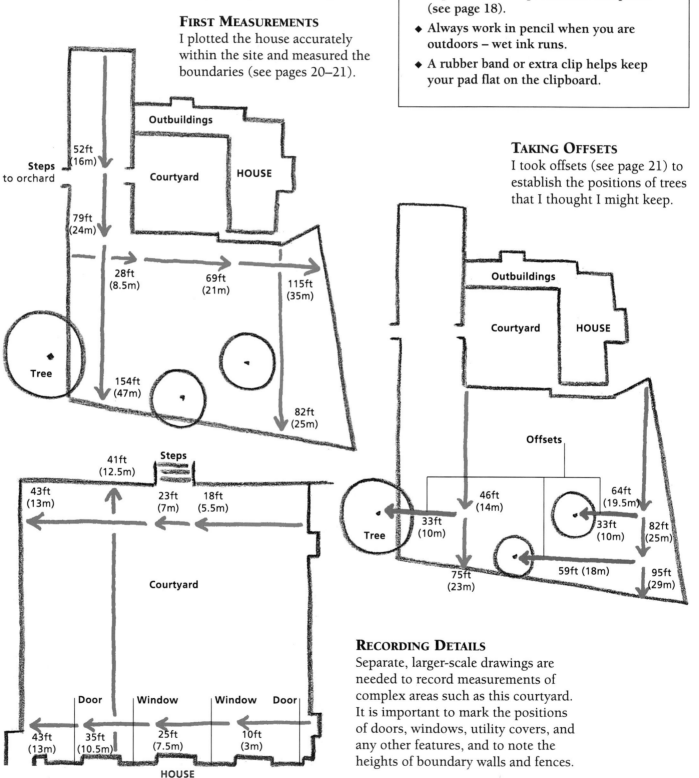

FIRST MEASUREMENTS
I plotted the house accurately within the site and measured the boundaries (see pages 20–21).

PRACTICAL TIPS

◆ You will need a tape measure, pegs to hold the tape and mark offsets, a pad on a clipboard, an HB pencil, and sharpener (see page 18).

◆ Always work in pencil when you are outdoors – wet ink runs.

◆ A rubber band or extra clip helps keep your pad flat on the clipboard.

TAKING OFFSETS
I took offsets (see page 21) to establish the positions of trees that I thought I might keep.

RECORDING DETAILS
Separate, larger-scale drawings are needed to record measurements of complex areas such as this courtyard. It is important to mark the positions of doors, windows, utility covers, and any other features, and to note the heights of boundary walls and fences.

Quartered squares will allow me to design this area in finer detail but still using a grid

The main unit of the grid based on the combined width of a door and a bay

Quartered
squares will
allow me to
design this
area in finer
detail but still
using a grid

The main unit
of the grid
based on the
combined
width of a
door and
a bay

CHOOSING THE GRID

The back of the house has a visual rhythm of door–bay–bay–door that divides the facade into four equal elements. I shall use this as the basis of my grid, though I can foresee it will need adapting for the courtyard area (see pages 14–15).

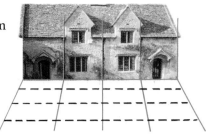

QUARTERING THE SQUARES

The grid squares are unwieldy in relation to the courtyard. To give myself more flexibility I quartered them.

DRAWING GRIDS

To work as I have done here, lay a sheet of tracing paper over your survey and draw the first lines of the grid, which are those that divide the house. The distance between these lines gives you the size of the grid square so that you can complete the square. Extend the grid until it covers the entire plan.

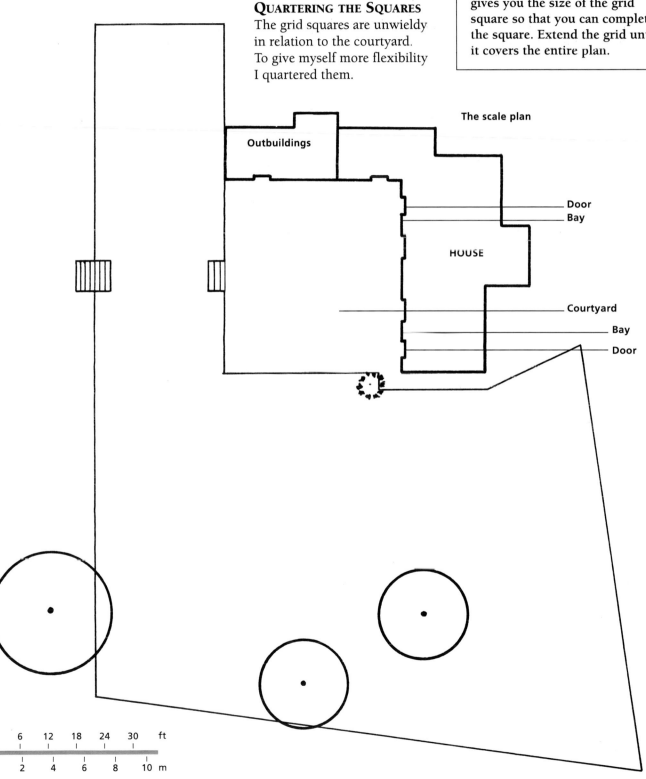

The scale plan

Outbuildings

Door
Bay

HOUSE

Courtyard

Bay

Door

| 0 | 6 | 12 | 18 | 24 | 30 | ft |

| 0 | 2 | 4 | 6 | 8 | 10 m |

PLANNING THE COURTYARD

THE COURTYARD IS THE CORE of this garden, and the obvious place to start; the rest of the design will develop from it. I decided to give the courtyard a strong center. Using quartered grid squares (see page 33) enabled me to experiment with shapes, while bearing in mind the practicalities of access.

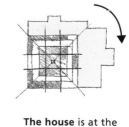 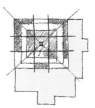

The house is at the side on the survey

I turned the plan 90° to design the courtyard

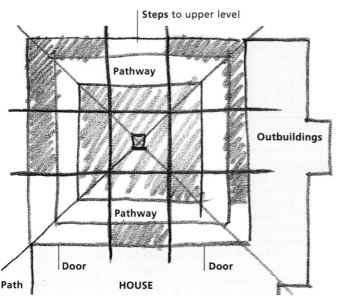

Steps to upper level

Pathway

Pathway

Outbuildings

Door   Door

Path   HOUSE

FIRST THOUGHTS

This design allows easy access to the house, the out-buildings, the path round the side of the house, and the steps to the garden's upper level. It is practical, but dull.

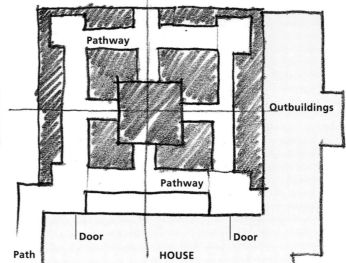

Pathway

Pathway

Outbuildings

Door   Door

Path   HOUSE

SECOND THOUGHTS

By cutting up the design further, I was able to create a complex, symmetrical pattern. This was interesting, but altogether too grand for the style of the house.

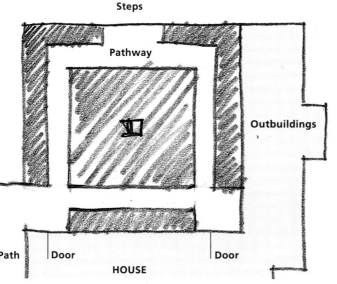

Steps

Pathway

Outbuildings

Path   Door   Door

HOUSE

RETHINKING

I rejected the over-formal pattern and made access to the buildings, path, and steps easier. An improvement: it is clean and focused, but still unexciting.

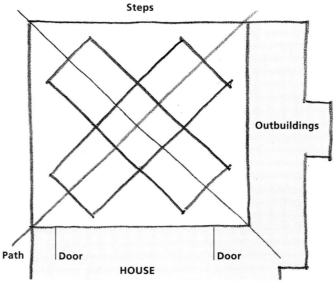

Steps

Outbuildings

Path   Door   Door

HOUSE

NEAR A SOLUTION

I turned the grid 45°. This results in some odd corners and no circulatory system as yet, but is interesting. I will try joining up the outer corners of the cross shape.

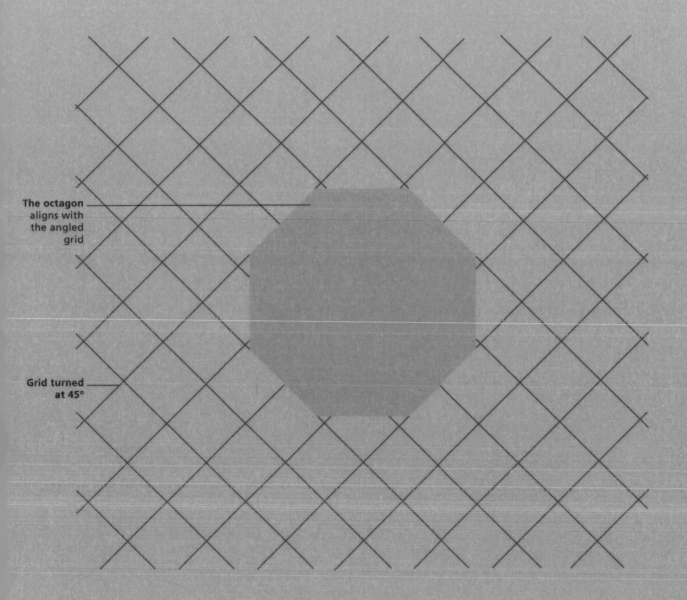

The octagon aligns with the angled grid

Grid turned at 45°

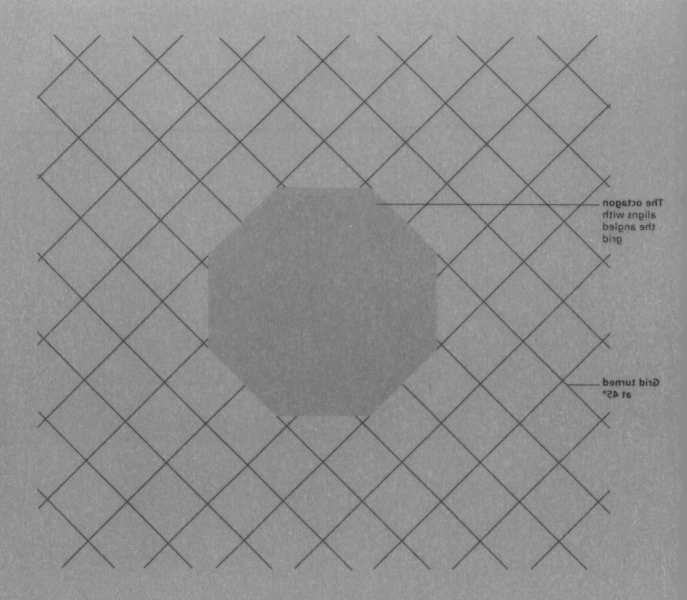

The octagon
aligns with
the angled
grid

Grid turned
at 45°

FROM CONCEPT TO COMPLETION

The cross shape is transformed into an octagon which allows a focal point in the center, easy access all around, and planting against the walls.

A PROFESSIONAL TOUCH

To plan a feature such as this octagonal courtyard it is a great help if the grid is angled through 45°. This produces diagonal lines with which to align the edges of the octagon.

```
0    3    6    9    12   ft
0    1    2    3    4  m
```

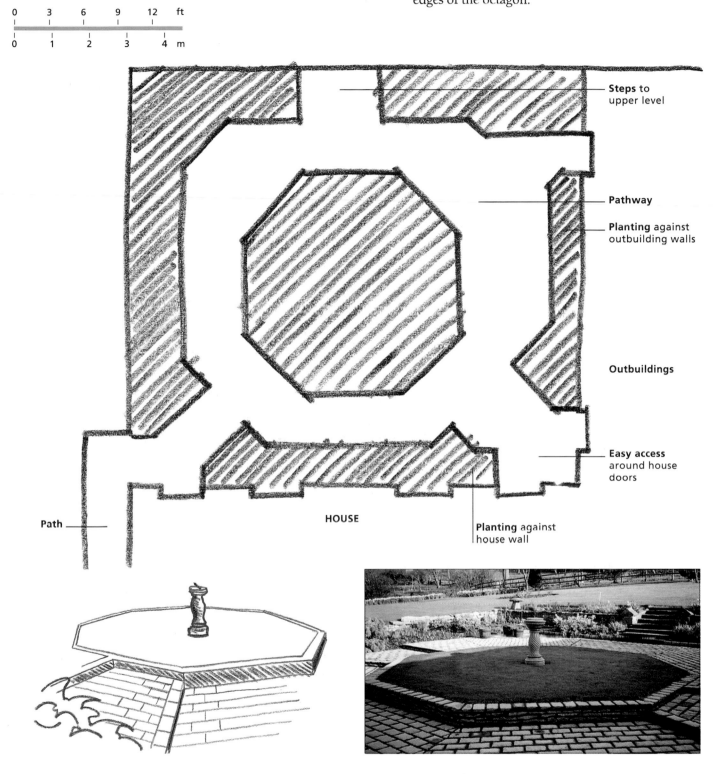

Steps to upper level

Pathway

Planting against outbuilding walls

Outbuildings

Easy access around house doors

Path

HOUSE

Planting against house wall

DETAILING THE DESIGN

Having decided upon the octagon and determined its size, I drew this sketch to show my design for the steps that are needed to compensate for changes in level.

THE FINISHED COURTYARD

With the construction stage completed, I can now confirm that the two pairs of steps work well, changing the gentle slope of the courtyard into clearly defined levels.

DEVELOPING THE DESIGN

NOW THAT I HAVE RESOLVED the pattern of the courtyard, it is time to extend the concept over the rest of the whole site, experimenting with octagons, diagonals, and right angles. The courtyard pattern arose when I turned the grid at 45° to the house, and I will keep the grid at this angle for the rest of the garden.

REMEMBERING THE BRIEF

The garden designer should no longer work in the abstract, but plan specific garden features that will work with the limitations of the site, so I refer back to the site survey and lay the grid over it.

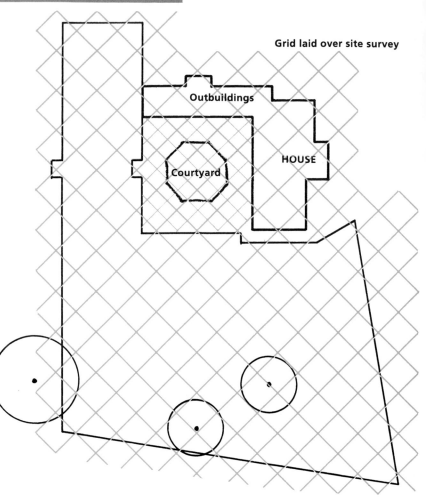

Grid laid over site survey

Outbuildings

Courtyard

HOUSE

Long view to summerhouse

Outbuildings

Long border

Courtyard

HOUSE

Upper lawn

Summerhouse and pool area

Existing tree in rough grass

Small orchard

Shrub screen

ANGLING THE GRID
I taped down the site survey with the grid laid across it at 45°, as with the courtyard. I reduced the courtyard design to the scale of the plan.

USING THE GRID'S ANGLES
Following the grid lines, I used the combination of diagonals and right angles that make up the courtyard design to define other areas of the garden (see left).

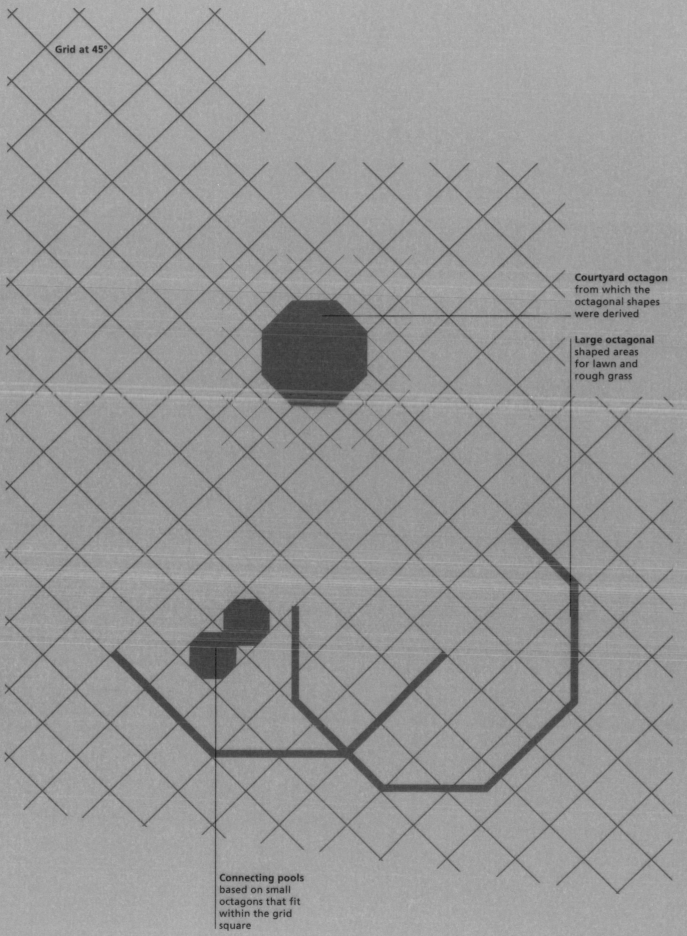

Grid at 45°

Courtyard octagon
from which the
octagonal shapes
were derived

Large octagonal
shaped areas
for lawn and
rough grass

Connecting pools
based on small
octagons that fit
within the grid
square

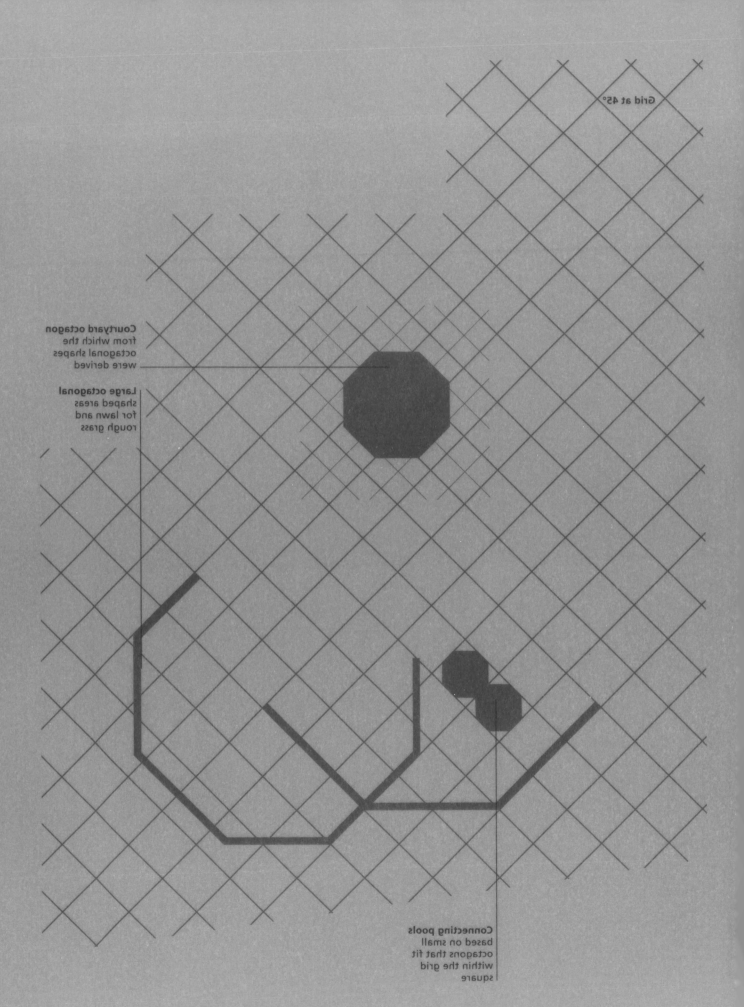

Courtyard octagon
from which the
octagonal shapes
were derived

Large octagonal
shaped areas
for lawn and
rough grass

Connecting pools
based on small
octagons that fit
within the grid
square

THE SKELETON DESIGN

I enlarged the octagon shape to supply the general pattern for the garden and reduced it to give shape to the rose garden, summerhouse, and connecting pools. The grid used is shown on the tracing paper overlay.

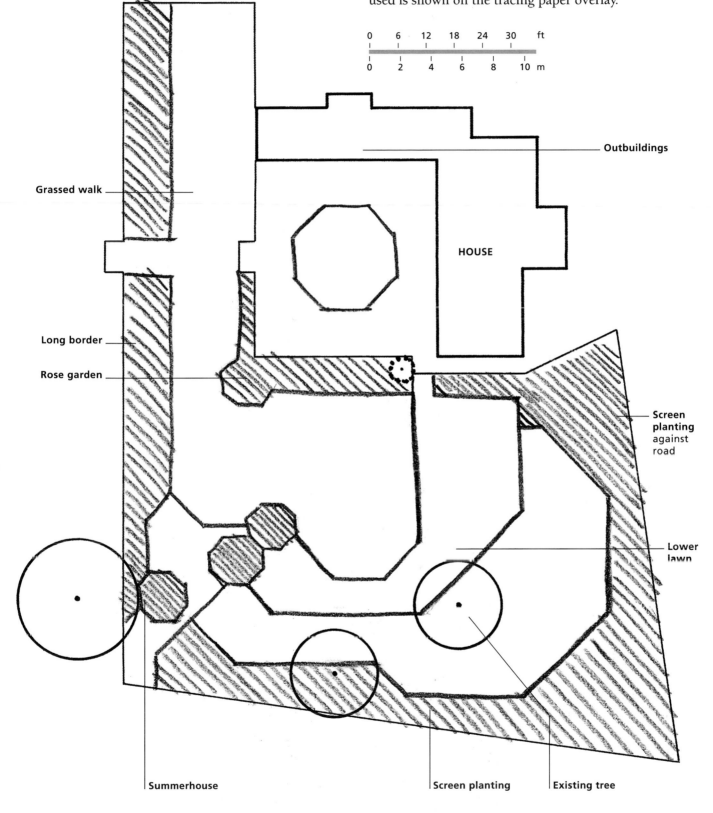

0	6	12	18	24	30	ft
0	2	4	6	8	10 m	

Outbuildings

Grassed walk

HOUSE

Long border

Rose garden

Screen planting against road

Lower lawn

Summerhouse

Screen planting

Existing tree

CHOOSING A STYLE

THE SHAPES YOU USE in a design should make the plan work for those who use the garden, but it is the styling of that design that makes the garden fit into its location. Plants are a major factor, but so are the choice of materials for paving and walling, the style of garden buildings, and the choice of garden furniture. All these elements should be in harmony with each other, and with the house and its wider location.

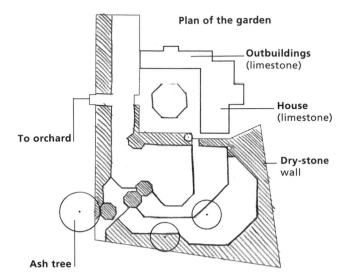

Plan of the garden

Outbuildings (limestone)

House (limestone)

To orchard

Dry-stone wall

Ash tree

PAVING AND WALLING

Select building materials that harmonize with the house and local tradition. Look at neighboring examples to help you decide on details of construction. For this case-study garden, dry-stone walling was the natural choice to match the limestone of adjacent buildings.

Sawed sandstone

Dressed sandstone

Limestone

Irregular paving

Concrete textures

Artificial stone

STYLES OF FENCING

Urban fences are used to screen out the neighbors and act as a form of security and are therefore likely to be solid. In the country, their purpose is to restrict animals, so open styles are adequate, perhaps modified with chicken wire where necessary.

Picket fencing

Hurdle fencing

GARDEN STRUCTURES

These should always be built to suit the house and the local style as far as possible. In this case study, the architect based the shape of the summerhouse (see page 43) on the form of an adjacent building and chose limestone to blend in with the surrounding structures.

CONTAINERS

Choose containers that have simple but pleasing outlines and are made in materials that are sympathetic to the surroundings. In a cottage garden, such as this, classical urns would be incongruous.

Unglazed container

Baskets can be painted or left plain, but need to be lined

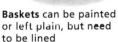

Studio pots are decorative in their own right

Terra-cotta pots should be frostproof

Wooden half-barrels must be kept damp

GARDEN FURNITURE

Both appearance and comfort matter when you choose furniture. Classic, simple benches and tables look good anywhere, but beware vibrant colors. Darker shades of paint and stain or plain, natural wood are more appropriate in a country setting.

Elegant seating suits formal gardens

Single chairs are easier to move than benches

Folding tables store away in winter

Simple forms work best in most gardens

VISUALIZING THE DESIGN

EVEN IF YOU ARE designing your own garden and have a firm idea of what you want, it is a good idea to sketch key areas and features to establish the concepts that guided the plan. Notice that open spaces (in this case lawns) are as important as planted spaces; I aim to create a visual balance between them.

FOCAL POINTS

There are two such features: the sundial in the center of the sunken courtyard, and the summerhouse.

THE SUMMERHOUSE

This terminates the mixed border and grass walk. It also echoes the roof lines of buildings beyond the site.

THE COURTYARD

This is how the courtyard and house will look seen from the summerhouse across the twin pools.

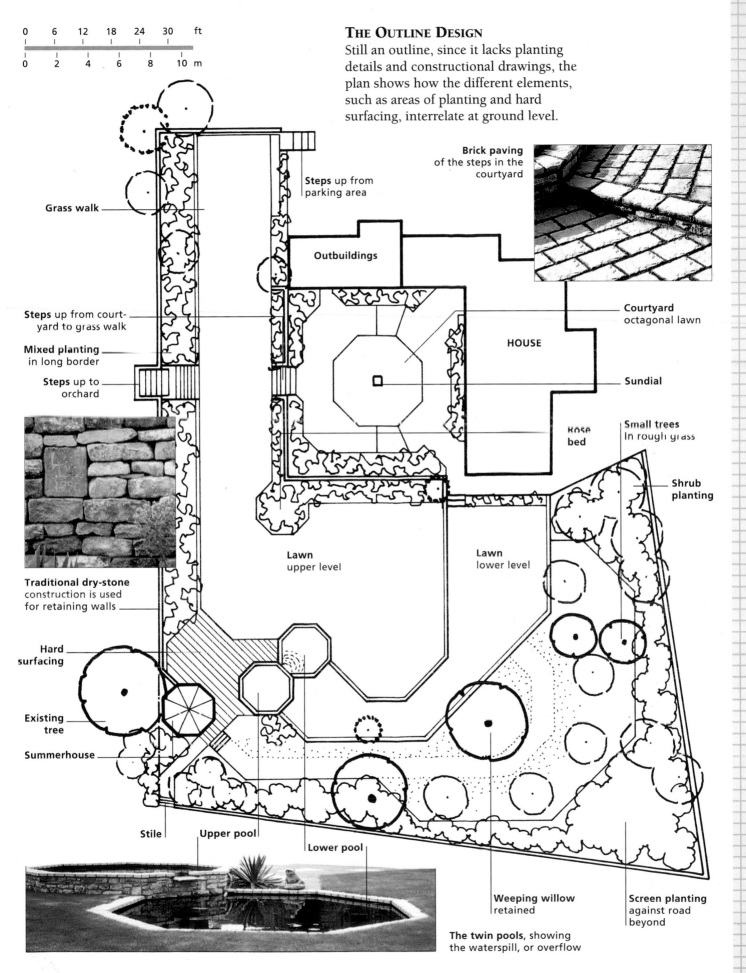

0 6 12 18 24 30 ft
0 2 4 6 8 10 m

THE OUTLINE DESIGN
Still an outline, since it lacks planting
details and constructional drawings, the
plan shows how the different elements,
such as areas of planting and hard
surfacing, interrelate at ground level.

Grass walk

Steps up from
parking area

Brick paving
of the steps in the
courtyard

Outbuildings

Steps up from court-
yard to grass walk

Mixed planting
in long border

Steps up to
orchard

Courtyard
octagonal lawn

HOUSE

Sundial

Rose
bed

Small trees
In rough grass

**Shrub
planting**

Traditional dry-stone
construction is used
for retaining walls

Lawn
upper level

Lawn
lower level

**Hard
surfacing**

**Existing
tree**

Summerhouse

Stile   **Upper pool**

Lower pool

Weeping willow
retained

Screen planting
against road
beyond

The twin pools, showing
the waterspill, or overflow

PLANNING TO BUILD

I DESIGNED THE LINKED OCTAGONAL POOLS to work with the summerhouse, which is also octagonal, strengthening the visual theme set in the courtyard. The upper pool is raised, whereas the lower pool is just below ground level. Their relationship exploits the natural slope of the site.

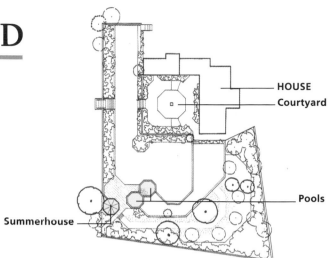

HOUSE
Courtyard
Pools
Summerhouse

THE POOLS

The linked pools are the most demanding features in the garden's construction.

THE POOLS AS FEATURES
The pools, with the summerhouse, provide the principal focus of the main garden.

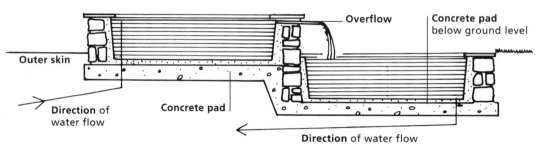

Overflow
Concrete pad
below ground level

Outer skin

Direction of water flow

Concrete pad

Direction of water flow

HOW THE POOLS WORK
The upper pool feeds the lower pool via an overflow, or waterspill. Water is pumped back to the top pool in a continuous circuit.

Outer skin
also serves as
an informal seat

BUILDING OCTAGONS
The plan of the summerhouse is laid out (above), while the pools are being excavated. The finished pools (below) are set off by the bold outline of a yucca.

THE SUMMERHOUSE

I planned the summerhouse to be the dominant feature of the main garden.

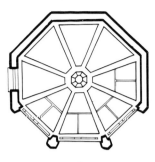

PLANNING THE SUMMERHOUSE
Quaint little garden buildings may be pretty but are impractical – I made sure the summerhouse was large enough to seat several people.

THE SUMMERHOUSE ELEVATION
The roofline of the summerhouse picks up the lines of the building that will be seen beyond it, across the road on the neighboring site.

GARDEN BUILDINGS

◆ Garden buildings are often too small in plan for their height, making them look ungainly. Disguise this fault by blending buildings into their background through careful planting.

◆ Experiment with wood stains – garden buildings do not need to be a standard yellowish brown.

◆ You may require a building permit for a permanent structure. Check first.

The materials of the summerhouse walls blend with the dry-stone walling in the foreground

The octagonal shapes of the pools echo the summerhouse

THE SUMMERHOUSE IN CONTEXT
With the summerhouse and pools built, you can see how the natural slope of the site makes the summerhouse dominant.

THE PLANTING PLAN

BACKING THE DECORATIVE PLANTS are tree and shrub masses which act as the permanent skeleton of the garden, giving it form and structure. They also mold the garden's views by blocking out unwanted features outside it, and they have a third function in sheltering the more tender plants within. I like to think of plants in masses; too many single specimens produce a staccato, restless effect.

VIEWPOINTS
Planting plans should be thought out so that the result looks good from all key viewing points in the garden.

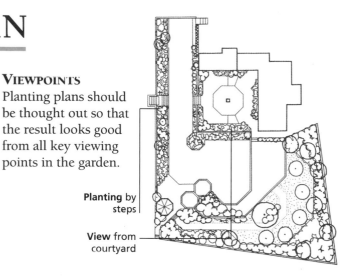

Planting by steps

View from courtyard

THE VIEW FROM THE COURTYARD
Layers of planting, shown below right in the early spring of the garden's second year, step up toward the summerhouse. The lower bed, being a year older than the higher ones, is fuller and more mature. I like to use a generous proportion of evergreen and "evergray" foliage to give fullness throughout the seasons. Flowers, when they appear, are a bonus.

PLANT DETAILING (BELOW)
At the corner of the steps up to the cherry orchard I set a bold mass of *Euphorbia wulfenii* – an evergreen which is at its best when it shows its spring flowers. The fleshy-leaved *Sedum* contrasts with the iris to the left and with the *Stachys* in front. Tall delphiniums, not yet showing, will soften the expanse of the new stone walls in summer.

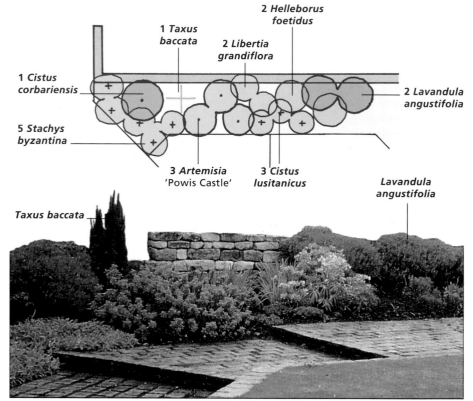

1 *Cistus corbariensis*

5 *Stachys byzantina*

1 *Taxus baccata*

2 *Libertia grandiflora*

2 *Helleborus foetidus*

3 *Artemisia* 'Powis Castle'

3 *Cistus lusitanicus*

2 *Lavandula angustifolia*

Taxus baccata

Lavandula angustifolia

Iris 'Jane Philips'

Euphorbia wulfenii

5 *Delphinium* mixed (not yet visible)

3 *Euphorbia wulfenii*

1 *Rosa moyesii*

5 *Sedum spectabile*

5 *Iris* 'Jane Philips'

2 *Stachys byzantina*

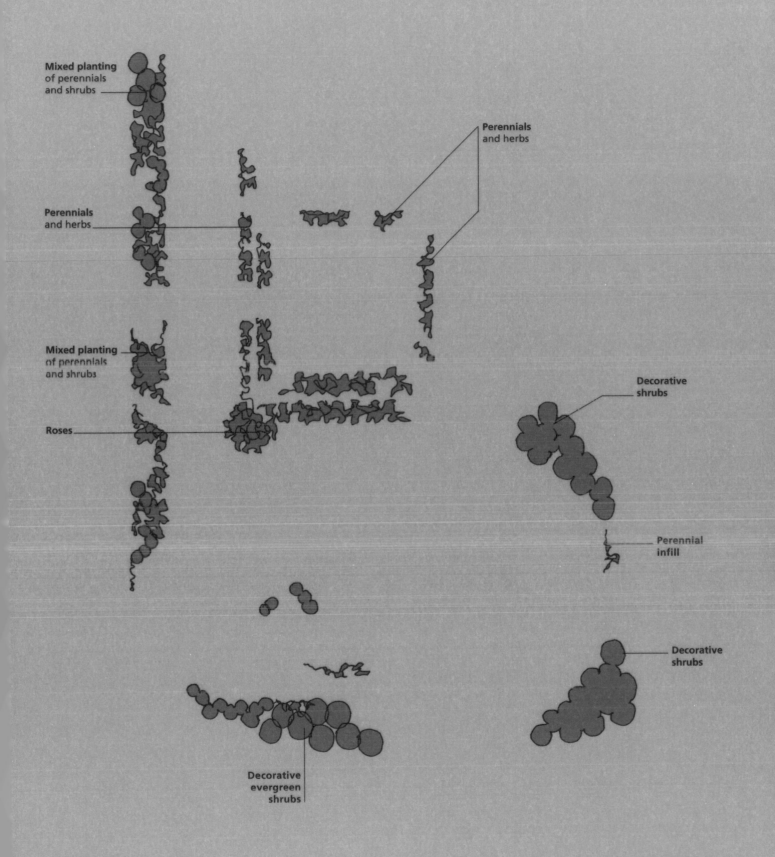

Mixed planting
of perennials
and shrubs

**Perennials
and herbs**

**Perennials
and herbs**

Mixed planting
of perennials
and shrubs

Roses

**Decorative
shrubs**

**Perennial
infill**

**Decorative
shrubs**

**Decorative
evergreen
shrubs**

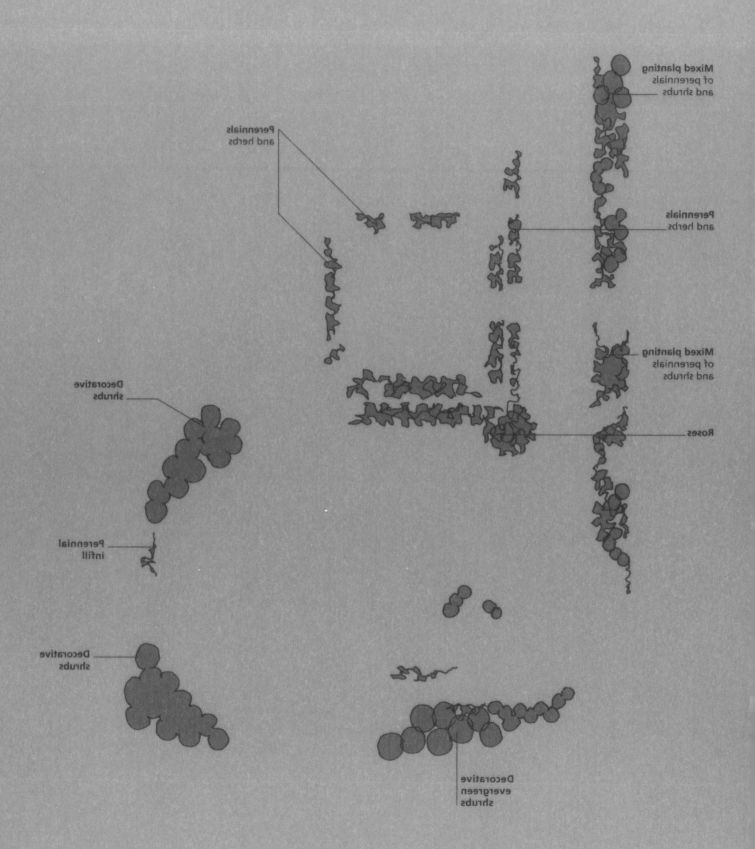

THE MASTER PLAN

The garden includes planting to provide permanent visual structure, act as a screen, and provide shelter. The decorative plants, including shrubs, perennials, roses, and herbs (all shown on the tracing paper) overlay the structural planting. The planting of the border by the grass walk is kept quite low to avoid obscuring the view up to the cherry orchard.

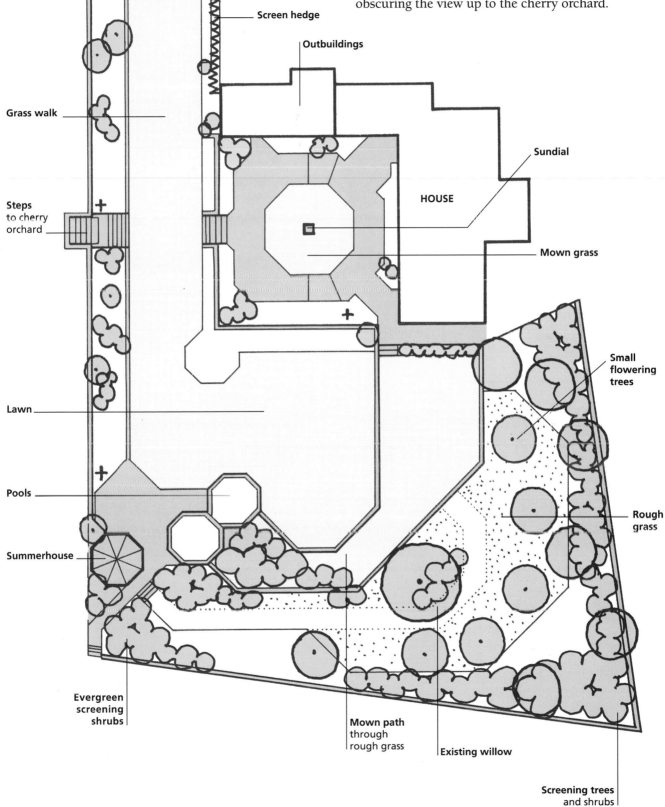

Screen hedge

Outbuildings

Grass walk

Sundial

HOUSE

Steps to cherry orchard

Mown grass

Small flowering trees

Lawn

Pools

Rough grass

Summerhouse

Evergreen screening shrubs

Mown path through rough grass

Existing willow

Screening trees and shrubs

THREE YEARS ON

IT TAKES ABOUT FIVE YEARS for plantings to mature enough to soften the design, producing the right balance between house, garden, and setting. These photographs, taken three years after the planting was complete, nonetheless show my intentions clearly: the garden is approaching early maturity.

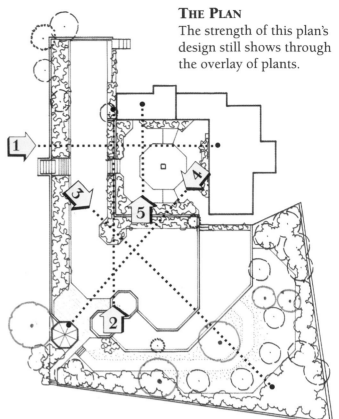

THE PLAN
The strength of this plan's design still shows through the overlay of plants.

THE GARDEN FROM THE CHERRY ORCHARD 1
In the foreground you see the steps from the orchard to the long walk. Beyond is the courtyard with its octagonal lawn from which the garden design developed.

THE VIEW FROM THE POOLS 2
From the top pool terrace, the development of the central rose bed and the mixed border on the left is apparent. Planting helps blend in the outbuildings.

THE SUMMERHOUSE [4]

From the courtyard (below) or the long walk, the summerhouse is a powerful focal point.

THE GARDEN IN ITS SETTING [3]

From the orchard there is an uninterrupted view of the countryside beyond the planting.

THE COURTYARD PLANTED [5]

Planting around the courtyard's grassed octagon softens and complements the structural elements.

HARMONY

You can now see how sympathy between new and old materials and building styles integrates the garden with its wider location, and how plants work to soften the composition and meld the garden into a whole.

THE
PLAN
PORTFOLIO

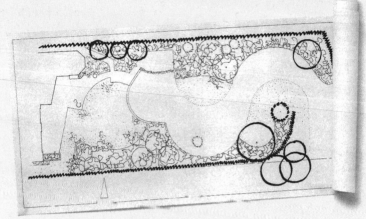

THE PLANS THAT FOLLOW have been chosen to
illustrate many different garden types,
the challenges they pose, and the design
solutions available.

KEY TO PLANS

Direction of north Viewpoint of sketch

1 A SMALL WALLED TOWN GARDEN

A COLLAGE OF RECTANGULAR SHAPES based on the proportions of the conservatory gave rise to a geometrical design with a pool at its center. The two finial balls set a classical tone, reinforced by clipped boxwood hedges that impose a strong sense of order on the looser plantings of shrubs behind them.

SITE NOTES

◆ In the lee of a 10ft (3m) wall, this is a sheltered, warm site.

◆ There are only two access points – a gate on the eastern side and the conservatory.

◆ The design brief calls for a water feature and a bench, to be given a classical-style interpretation.

◆ With so much going on in quite a small space – approximately 23 x 30ft (7 x 9m) – there is a risk of clutter, so grid selection will be crucial.

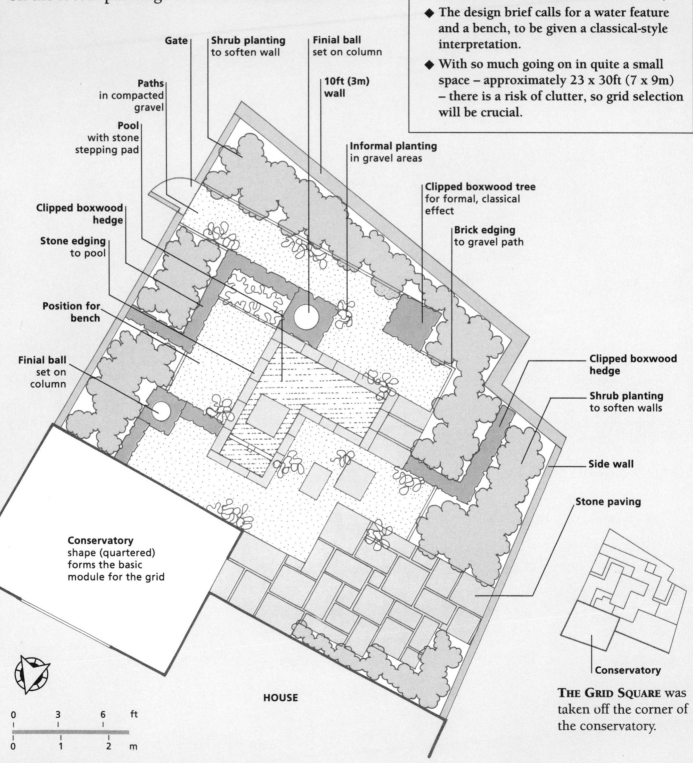

Gate

Shrub planting to soften wall

Finial ball set on column

Paths in compacted gravel

10ft (3m) wall

Pool with stone stepping pad

Informal planting in gravel areas

Clipped boxwood hedge

Clipped boxwood tree for formal, classical effect

Stone edging to pool

Brick edging to gravel path

Position for bench

Finial ball set on column

Clipped boxwood hedge

Shrub planting to soften walls

Side wall

Stone paving

Conservatory shape (quartered) forms the basic module for the grid

Conservatory

HOUSE

0   3   6   ft
0   1   2   m

THE GRID SQUARE was taken off the corner of the conservatory.

2 AN ENCLOSED SIDE GARDEN

THE SCALE OF THIS GARDEN derives from the large piece of statuary which is its focus and which is carefully related in scale to the high wall behind it. The garden is softened by a selection of shade-loving plants in the shadow of the south wall and brightened by colorful exotics in the sunny areas.

VIEW DOWN THE GARDEN, showing how the urn works as a focal point against the high boundary wall.

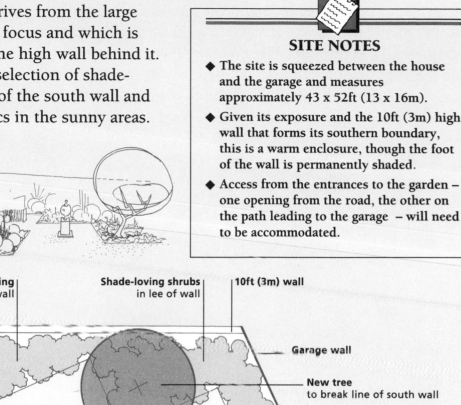

SITE NOTES

◆ The site is squeezed between the house and the garage and measures approximately 43 x 52ft (13 x 16m).

◆ Given its exposure and the 10ft (3m) high wall that forms its southern boundary, this is a warm enclosure, though the foot of the wall is permanently shaded.

◆ Access from the entrances to the garden – one opening from the road, the other on the path leading to the garage – will need to be accommodated.

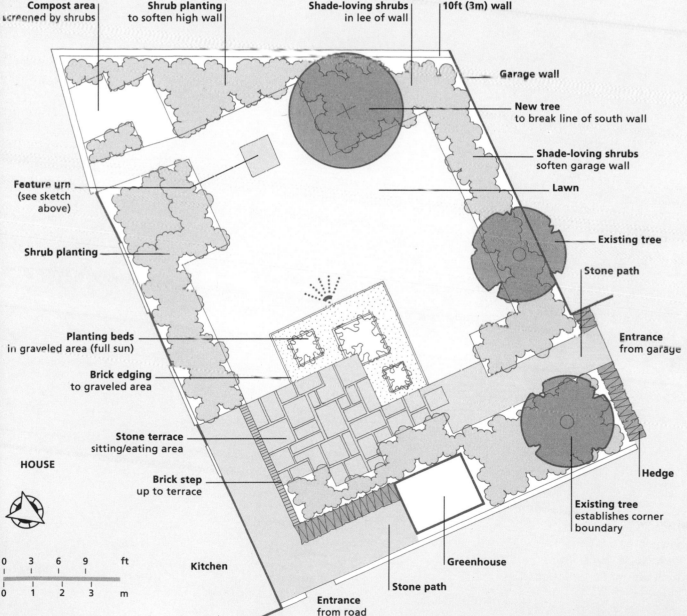

Compost area screened by shrubs

Shrub planting to soften high wall

Shade-loving shrubs in lee of wall

10ft (3m) wall

Garage wall

New tree to break line of south wall

Shade-loving shrubs soften garage wall

Lawn

Feature urn (see sketch above)

Existing tree

Stone path

Shrub planting

Entrance from garage

Planting beds in graveled area (full sun)

Brick edging to graveled area

Stone terrace sitting/eating area

HOUSE

Brick step up to terrace

Hedge

Existing tree establishes corner boundary

Kitchen

Greenhouse

Stone path

| 0 | 3 | 6 | 9 | ft |
| 0 | 1 | 2 | 3 | m |

Entrance from road

3 A RECTANGULAR SUBURBAN SITE

THIS TYPICAL RECTANGULAR PLOT is at the rear of a suburban house. Evolving the design at 45° to the house adds an illusion of width, which is reinforced by breaking the site into a sequence of individual "rooms" defined by plant masses, brick edging, and contrasting surfaces. Though the design actually consists of formal square areas, a meandering effect is created.

SITE NOTES

◆ The plot is not long – only about 65ft (20m) – so it makes sense to plan the garden as a sequence of "rooms" to suggest length.

◆ Setting the plan at an angle to the house will make the garden appear wider.

◆ For the owners to be able to enjoy the afternoon sun, a seating area needs to be created at the rear, clear of the house.

Existing tree

Compacted gravel
contrasts with
adjacent brick

Storage shed
hidden by planting

Brick seating terrace
to catch afternoon sun

Existing hedge
retained

Planting of shrubs
for fall/winter color

Step made of
bricks laid on edge

Existing
hedge

Brick
edge/step

Paving slabs

Fountain

Cobbled area

Lawn

Lawn

Paving
to side access

Herb garden
convenient for
kitchen

Kitchen

Step
made of
bricks laid
on edge

Mixed planting

Brick-laid terrace
for morning sun

Fence

Door

Door

HOUSE

0 3 6 9 ft
0 1 2 3 m

BLOCK PLAN
showing the
interlocking shapes from
which the garden is designed.

4 A GARDEN IN A HOLLOW

BUILDING A RETAINING WALL toward the perimeter allows the part of the garden closest to the house to be leveled. The wall is made thicker to provide seating near the conservatory, whose shape is echoed in the central bed and picked up in the lines of the terrace and both lawns. Defined geometrical shapes such as this tend to work well in small gardens, where loose curves often look weak.

SITE NOTES

◆ The garden rises by more than 3ft (1m) from the house to the southern and eastern boundaries.

◆ The octagonal conservatory is the dominant feature of both the side and rear gardens. It is an obvious shape to develop into the design.

◆ The brief includes a requirement to maximize the lawn and terrace areas.

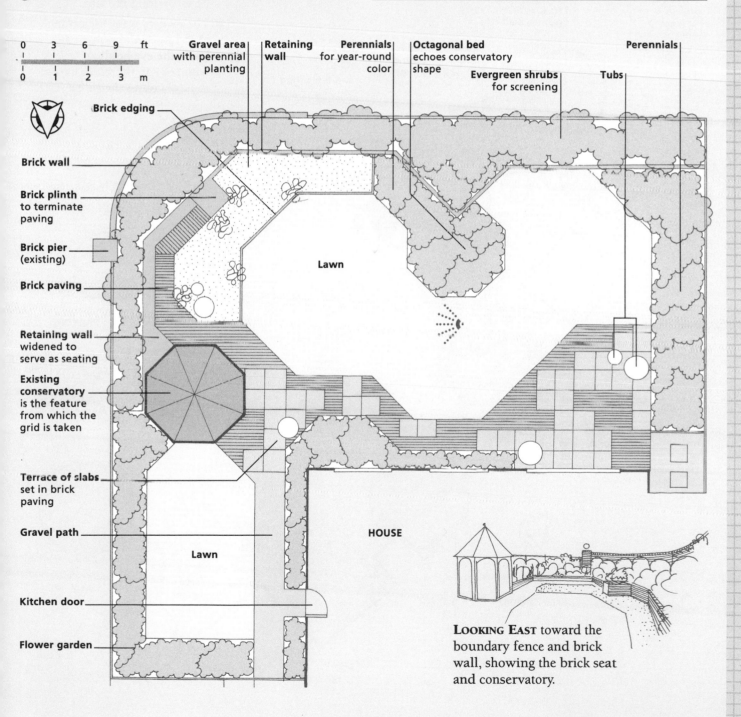

Scale:
```
0    3    6    9    ft
|    |    |    |
0    1    2    3    m
```

Gravel area with perennial planting

Retaining wall

Perennials for year-round color

Octagonal bed echoes conservatory shape

Evergreen shrubs for screening

Perennials

Tubs

Brick edging

Brick wall

Brick plinth to terminate paving

Brick pier (existing)

Brick paving

Retaining wall widened to serve as seating

Existing conservatory is the feature from which the grid is taken

Terrace of slabs set in brick paving

Gravel path

Lawn

Lawn

HOUSE

Kitchen door

Flower garden

LOOKING EAST toward the boundary fence and brick wall, showing the brick seat and conservatory.

5 A SCREENED GARDEN

SCREENING OUT THE NEIGHBORS is more easily said than done – an obvious screen makes one wonder what is behind it. The solution here is to draw the eye into the site with the heavy patterning of flower beds set into the run of brick paving; shrubs and perennials will be able to flop over the terracing without impeding the lawnmower. The ornamental tree by the entrance to the parking area acts as a secondary focus.

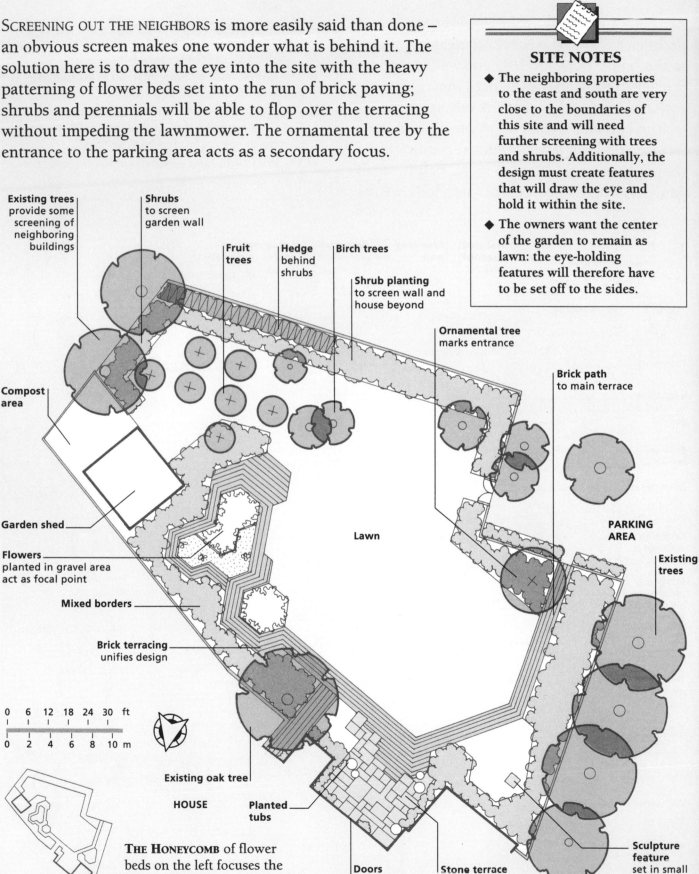

Existing trees provide some screening of neighboring buildings

Shrubs to screen garden wall

Fruit trees

Hedge behind shrubs

Birch trees

Shrub planting to screen wall and house beyond

Ornamental tree marks entrance

Brick path to main terrace

Compost area

Garden shed

Flowers planted in gravel area act as focal point

Mixed borders

Brick terracing unifies design

PARKING AREA

Existing trees

Lawn

0 6 12 18 24 30 ft

0 2 4 6 8 10 m

Existing oak tree

HOUSE

Planted tubs

Doors to terrace

Stone terrace

Sculpture feature set in small lawn

THE HONEYCOMB of flower beds on the left focuses the garden pattern.

6 AN URBAN CORNER SITE

THE HOUSE HAS A FORMAL FACADE, but the garden's shape is irregular. Squaring up the lawn and terrace goes some way to reconciling the two, with a tree introduced to create a line of vision from the house. From the seating area the focus is the sycamore, with the pool, backed by water plants, as a counterpoint.

THE LARGE SYCAMORE is balanced by areas of interest created at lower levels in the garden.

SITE NOTES

◆ The plot is dominated by a large sycamore on the western flank.

◆ The owners require a lawn and a wading pool for their children. They also wish to have a paved seating area where they can enjoy the sun.

◆ A line of vision needs to be created from the house and another from the seating area: the sycamore is an obvious focal point for the latter.

| 0 | 3 | 6 | 9 | ft |
| 0 | 1 | 2 | 3 | m |

Sculpture

New tree to terminate view from house

Brick seating wall

Wading pool

Water planting

Existing trees

Shrub planting to soften wall

Dominant sycamore

Trellis screen

Brick seating wall

Shrubs to screen fence

Lawn

Slab-paved seating area

New seating area (brick-paved)

New trees

Doors to terrace

Planted tubs

HOUSE

Shaded brick seating area

55

7 A GARDEN WITH AN OPEN VIEW

THE LINE OF THE STEPS down from the terrace to the lawn radiates from the raised pool, which is the center of the pattern, and directs the eye toward the break in the hedge that reveals the paddock and horses. The planting on the southern and western boundaries provides valuable wind shelter.

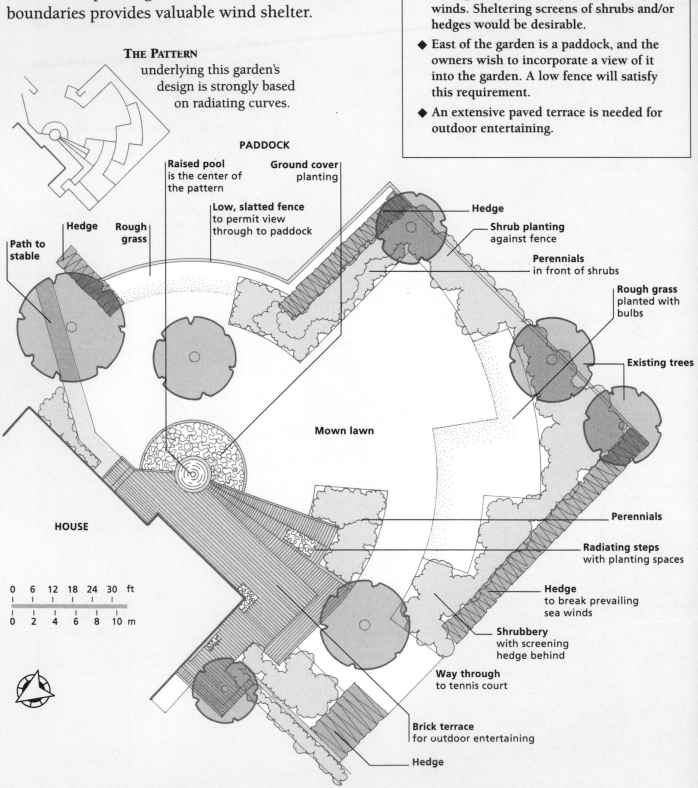

THE PATTERN underlying this garden's design is strongly based on radiating curves.

PADDOCK

Raised pool is the center of the pattern

Ground cover planting

Low, slatted fence to permit view through to paddock

Hedge

Shrub planting against fence

Perennials in front of shrubs

Rough grass planted with bulbs

Existing trees

Hedge

Rough grass

Path to stable

Mown lawn

Perennials

Radiating steps with planting spaces

Hedge to break prevailing sea winds

Shrubbery with screening hedge behind

Way through to tennis court

HOUSE

0 6 12 18 24 30 ft
0 2 4 6 8 10 m

Brick terrace for outdoor entertaining

Hedge

8 A COUNTRY COURTYARD

THREE CHANGES OF LEVEL are incorporated in this squared layout; the collage of patterns is old stone, granite setts (paving blocks), and plantings of mainly culinary herbs. The areas of paving are punctuated with wooden tubs planted with bright annuals for summer color.

SITE NOTES

◆ Old farm buildings on either side of the courtyard are to be retained.

◆ Though it has an unfavourable exposure, the site is enclosed by buildings and walls and is therefore very well sheltered.

◆ The garden slopes up from the house to the gate – steps will resolve this.

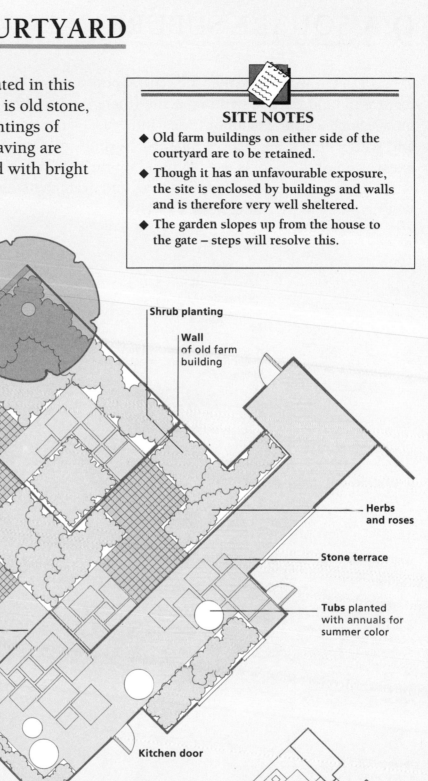

Existing tree

Shrub planting to soften wall

Sculpture to focus view from the house

Perimeter wall

Granite setts

Stone slabs

Gate to parking area

Step up

Shrubs

Step up

Granite setts

Herbs and roses

Shrub planting

Wall of old farm building

Herbs and roses

Stone terrace

Tubs planted with annuals for summer color

Kitchen door

HOUSE

Wall of old farm building

| 0 | 3 | 6 | 9 | 12 | ft |
| 0 | 1 | 2 | 3 | 4 | m |

THE GRID underlying this layout was based on the proportions of the house, then subdivided into smaller areas.

9 A SQUARE SUBURBAN PLOT

THE BULL'S-EYE PATTERN makes the central pool a powerful feature to hold the eye within the site (there is a very limited view). Such a strong geometric design needs a fairly wide site and works only if heavily overplanted. Surplus soil from the excavation of the pool is used to build up the border at the end of the garden. When planted with trees and evergreens, this will help block out traffic noise as well.

THIS PATTERN contrasts modernity in layout with very soft planting designed to encourage birds.

0 3 6 9 12 ft
0 1 2 3 4 m

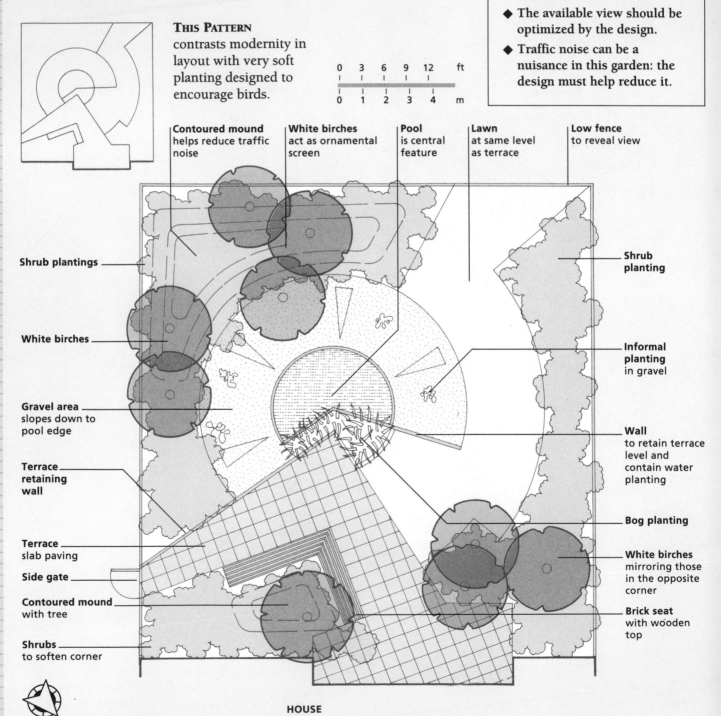

Contoured mound helps reduce traffic noise

White birches act as ornamental screen

Pool is central feature

Lawn at same level as terrace

Low fence to reveal view

Shrub plantings

White birches

Gravel area slopes down to pool edge

Terrace retaining wall

Terrace slab paving

Side gate

Contoured mound with tree

Shrubs to soften corner

Shrub planting

Informal planting in gravel

Wall to retain terrace level and contain water planting

Bog planting

White birches mirroring those in the opposite corner

Brick seat with wooden top

HOUSE

10 A SPLIT-LEVEL GARDEN

MANY OLDER ATTACHED HOUSES have rear gardens that are approached from a basement area subsequently opened out to increase light to a remodeled kitchen. The first task here is to improve the basement seating area. The second is to angle the lawn-level pattern so that the terrace faces the sun. The third is to fix the eye with a leveled area in the bank created by surplus soil at the end.

THE VIEW down into the garden from a tall townhouse can vary greatly according to which floor you look from: the design should take this into account.

Existing tree

Raised graveled area with informal planting

Large pots attract the eye

Brick seating area facing afternoon sun

Shrubs

Climbers

Shrubs to disguise end fence

Sculpture feature to draw the eye

Bank of soil

Lawn

Fence masked by shrubs

Brick edging to lawn

HOUSE

Kitchen door

Flight of steps from lower terrace to upper garden

Retaining wall

Barbecue area

Brick lower terrace with stone slabs interspersed

| 0 | 3 | 6 | ft |
| 0 | 1 | 2 | m |

SITE NOTES

◆ Surplus soil dug out when the basement area was extended was dumped at the end of the garden. This needs to be tidied into a secondary level of the main garden with a feature to draw the eye.

◆ The line of the garden is due east: a seating area facing south will have to be made.

◆ Access is from the basement only – there are no steps down from the raised ground floor of the house.

11 A RIVERSIDE TERRACE

THIS TERRACE WITH A RIVER VIEW is severely overlooked by a neighboring building. Strong ground detailing with a small water feature and a pergola all deflect the eye from the neighboring property. For maximum impact the pergola is sited where the east-west and north-south axes meet, and its octagonal design reflects the pattern of the bay windows looking on to the garden. Planting tall shrubs behind the pergola strengthens the concept.

SITE NOTES

◆ The terrace has an excellent river view, but its enjoyment is spoiled by a tall neighboring building, which overlooks the terrace to the point of domination.

◆ An unplanted gravel area at the foot of the garden is needed to provide an unrestricted view across the river.

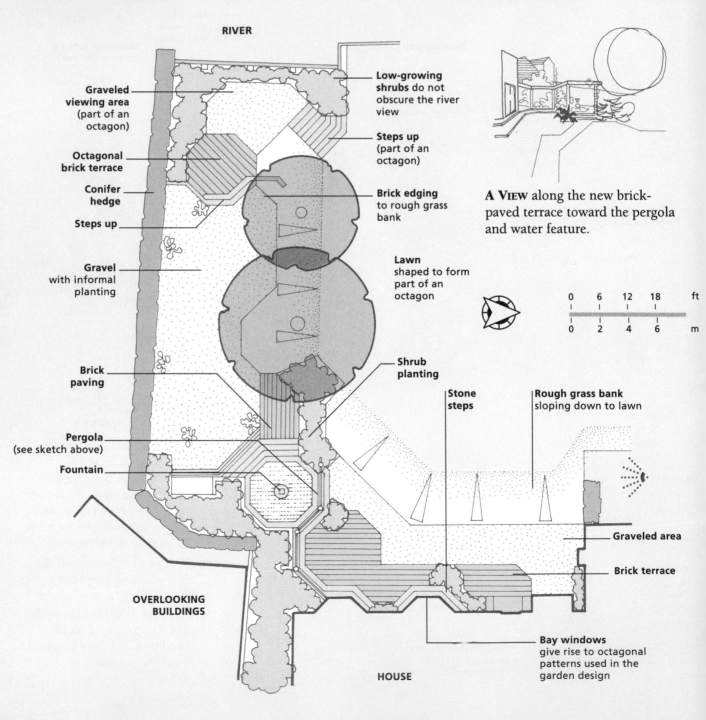

RIVER

Graveled viewing area (part of an octagon)

Octagonal brick terrace

Conifer hedge

Steps up

Gravel with informal planting

Brick paving

Pergola (see sketch above)

Fountain

Low-growing shrubs do not obscure the river view

Steps up (part of an octagon)

Brick edging to rough grass bank

Lawn shaped to form part of an octagon

Shrub planting

Stone steps

Rough grass bank sloping down to lawn

Graveled area

Brick terrace

Bay windows give rise to octagonal patterns used in the garden design

OVERLOOKING BUILDINGS

HOUSE

A VIEW along the new brick-paved terrace toward the pergola and water feature.

| 0 | 6 | 12 | 18 | ft |
| 0 | 2 | 4 | 6 | m |

12 A SEASIDE FRONT GARDEN

A WINDBREAK does not make a successful feature – however well it serves its purpose – in an ordinary-sized garden. The visual impact of this plan for a windy coastal garden comes from a strong ground pattern, expressed in brick, grass, and gravel, stepping up three times to the front door. Planted pots on a brick pad in the gravel provide a focus from the street entry as well as from the house.

0   3   6   9   ft
0   1   2   3   m

Mixed planting

Shrub planting to soften wall

Hedge (windbreak)

Wall (windbreak)

Lawn

Shrubs to soften wall

Planted pots on brick pad

Graveled area with loose planting

Granite sett edging

Tiled threshold

Perennials

Brick paving level 3

Brick paving level 2

Garden entrance from driveway

Brick paving level 1

Entrance

HOUSE

Shrub planting

A Strong Ground Pattern works with the house's proportions to create interest. The layout allows a wide approach to the front door.

SITE NOTES

◆ The exposure is very windy, so some sort of protective enclosure is essential. It must not become oppressive, however – even in this modest space it will be necessary to create interest within the plot.

◆ The bold windows that dominate the house are the basis for the grid.

13 AN ANGULAR GARDEN

USING A SIMPLE GEOMETRY deriving from the plan of the house, the rear garden resolves itself into a paved forecourt, brick terrace, and lawn, bounded by low shrubs that will not obscure the attractive view to the south. Side areas are maximized by leveling near the house and pushing the rising ground back behind retaining walls. A path is created to zigzag through the stepped-up north border.

SITE NOTES

◆ The rear of the house looks south to a fine view, which should be emphasized.

◆ The north-facing front garden and the areas to the sides of the house rise toward the boundaries and will need retaining to create some level space.

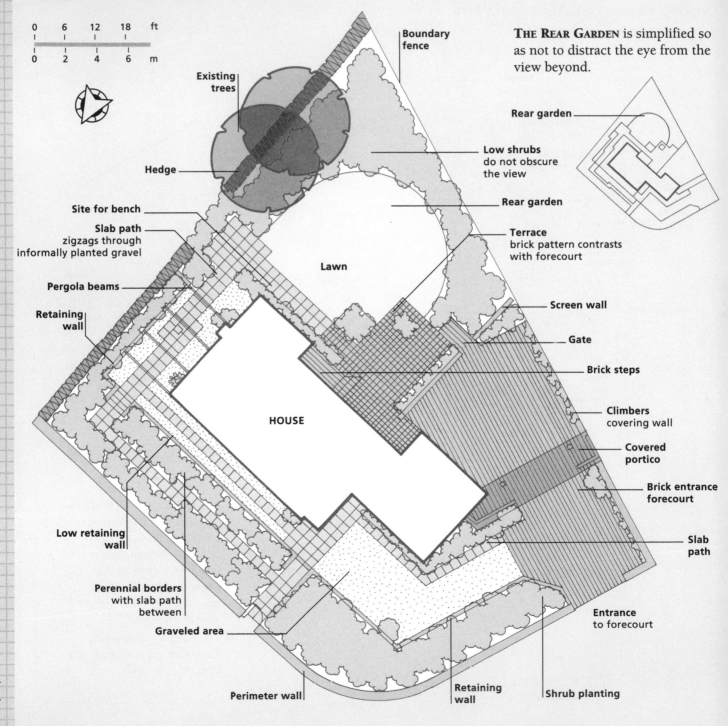

0   6   12   18   ft
0   2   4   6   m

Existing trees

Boundary fence

THE REAR GARDEN is simplified so as not to distract the eye from the view beyond.

Rear garden

Hedge

Low shrubs do not obscure the view

Site for bench

Rear garden

Slab path zigzags through informally planted gravel

Lawn

Terrace brick pattern contrasts with forecourt

Pergola beams

Screen wall

Retaining wall

Gate

Brick steps

HOUSE

Climbers covering wall

Covered portico

Brick entrance forecourt

Low retaining wall

Slab path

Perennial borders with slab path between

Graveled area

Entrance to forecourt

Perimeter wall

Retaining wall

Shrub planting

14 A BANKED GARDEN

THE FIRST TASK is to extend the lower terrace by pushing the bank back behind a retaining brick wall. This allows for improved access by new steps to the upper level, where a new second terrace takes advantage of the view down over the cottage.

THE SHELTERED paved terrace at the lower level of the garden.

SITE NOTES

◆ The cottage nestles into the bank that surrounds it on the eastern and southern sides. The garden proper is on a level with the second-floor rooms.

◆ The terrace, protected by the bank to the east and north, and by the cottage on the south and west, is remarkably sheltered and sunny.

◆ Lawnmower access needs to be provided from the rear garden past the side of the cottage to the front lawn (not shown).

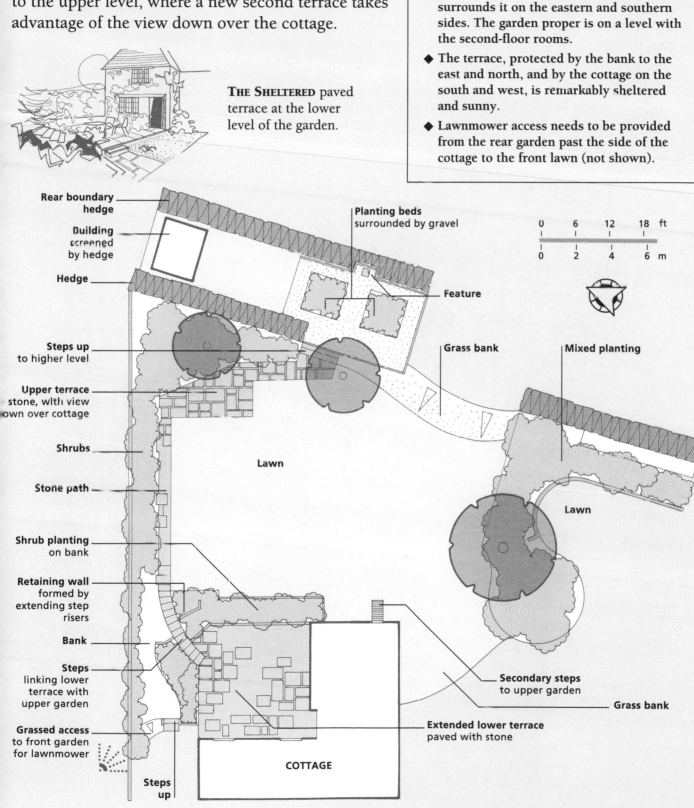

Rear boundary hedge

Building screened by hedge

Hedge

Steps up to higher level

Upper terrace stone, with view down over cottage

Shrubs

Stone path

Shrub planting on bank

Retaining wall formed by extending step risers

Bank

Steps linking lower terrace with upper garden

Grassed access to front garden for lawnmower

Steps up

Planting beds surrounded by gravel

Feature

Grass bank

Mixed planting

Lawn

Lawn

Secondary steps to upper garden

Grass bank

Extended lower terrace paved with stone

COTTAGE

0	6	12	18	ft
0	2	4	6	m

15 A ROADSIDE GARDEN SCREENED

WHEN IT WAS FIRST LAID OUT in the early 1900s, this garden was oriented toward the southwest. Now, to avoid the increased noise that comes from the road beyond the southern boundary, it makes sense to create a new principal terrace on the northwest side of the house, with twin views of a new flower garden to the north and the existing beeches to the west.

THE VIEW from the extended terrace by the house across the formal flower garden to the summerhouse.

SITE NOTES

◆ The road beyond the southern boundary has become noisy. An alternative seating area is required where the noise will be less intrusive.

◆ A shrub screen on the southern boundary will reduce noise and give shelter from the prevailing winds.

◆ A substantial asset of the existing garden is the fine group of large beech trees.

Shrub screen against road noise and prevailing winds

Existing large trees

Steps down to flower garden and lawns

Summerhouse

Orchard planting

Rough grass under trees planted with bulbs

Lawn

New formal beds in gravel surround

Existing tree

Mixed small trees and shrubs

Steps up to terrace

Original brick-paved terrace

Lawn

Boundary hedge

New extension to terrace shielded from road noise by projecting wing of the house

HOUSE

ROAD

Entrance to house

0 9 18 27 36 ft

0 3 6 9 12 m

16 A GARDEN FOR A FORMER STABLE

To HOLD THE EYE WITHIN THE SITE, a simple round lily pool is made the focal point of sweeping circular patterns, defined by yew and shrub hedges that help to obscure the garden buildings in the southeast corner and conceal the driveway. The sun terrace, positioned to give a view back to the former stable, functions as part of this pattern.

THE PATTERN of strong curves gives a sense of enclosure and focuses the eye on the central pool.

SITE NOTES
◆ The former stable – now a cottage – is a pretty building with a graceful church spire behind it. A south-facing terrace should be created to take advantage of this view.
◆ Other views from the garden are not especially attractive, so the eye needs to be retained within the site.

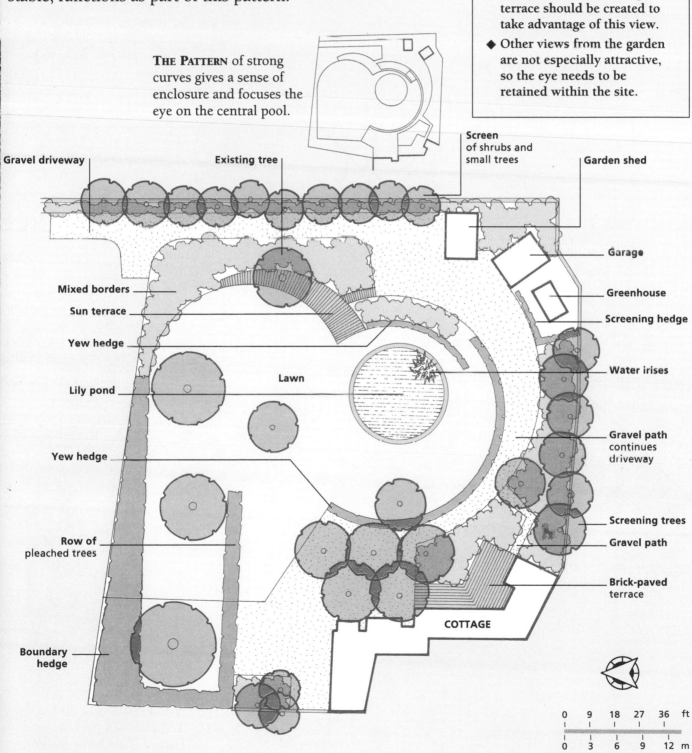

Gravel driveway

Existing tree

Screen of shrubs and small trees

Garden shed

Garage

Mixed borders

Sun terrace

Yew hedge

Lily pond

Yew hedge

Row of pleached trees

Boundary hedge

Greenhouse

Screening hedge

Water irises

Lawn

Gravel path continues driveway

Screening trees

Gravel path

Brick-paved terrace

COTTAGE

0	9	18	27	36	ft
0	3	6	9	12	m

17 A SMALL COURTYARD DESIGN

AN UPPER POOL TRICKLING INTO A LOWER ONE makes the feature, emphasized by a piece of sculpture, that holds the eye in the courtyard rather than allowing it to follow the lines of the birch upward. Low brick walls retain most of the planting at the edges of the site and provide casual seating. The brick paving matches the retaining walls, but the design is made less formal by introducing stone slabs.

SITE NOTES

- ◆ The white birch dominates the space and naturally draws the eye upward. A strong feature is necessary to hold the eye down.
- ◆ Doorways to the south, east, and west dictate the siting of a feature near the base of the birch tree.
- ◆ Paved space is required for eating outdoors in summer.

```
0   1   2   3   4   5  ft
|   |   |   |   |   |
|       |       |
0     0.5    1    1.5  m
```

Mixed planting
in raised bed

Seating area
is brick-paved, with
occasional stone slabs to
relieve the formality

STUDIO

Informal planting
in brick cutout

Low retaining wall

Door
from studio to
courtyard

Existing
large white
birch

Shrubs

Raised bed
planted with
shrubs

Upper
pool

Plinth
for intended
sculpture

Lower pool

Raised brick edge

Mixed shrub planting
in ground-level bed

Feature tree

Brick retaining wall
also serves for
seating

Entrance
to courtyard

Stone slabs
stepped down

Door
from house
to courtyard

HOUSE

Stone slab
acts as water course,
joining the pools

THE VERTICALS of the birch contrast with the horizontal planes of the water feature.

18 A PRIVATE TOWN GARDEN

CREATING PRIVACY IN A SMALL TOWN GARDEN is one of the classic garden design challenges. A light, skeletal metal arbor beneath an existing tree provides some screening from neighboring houses in this tall terrace. The eye is drawn to this structure across a foreground pattern of paving preceded by gravel heavily planted with herbs and shrub roses, and evergreens for winter interest in the shade.

THE NEW STRUCTURE as it appears from the ground floor rear rooms of the house.

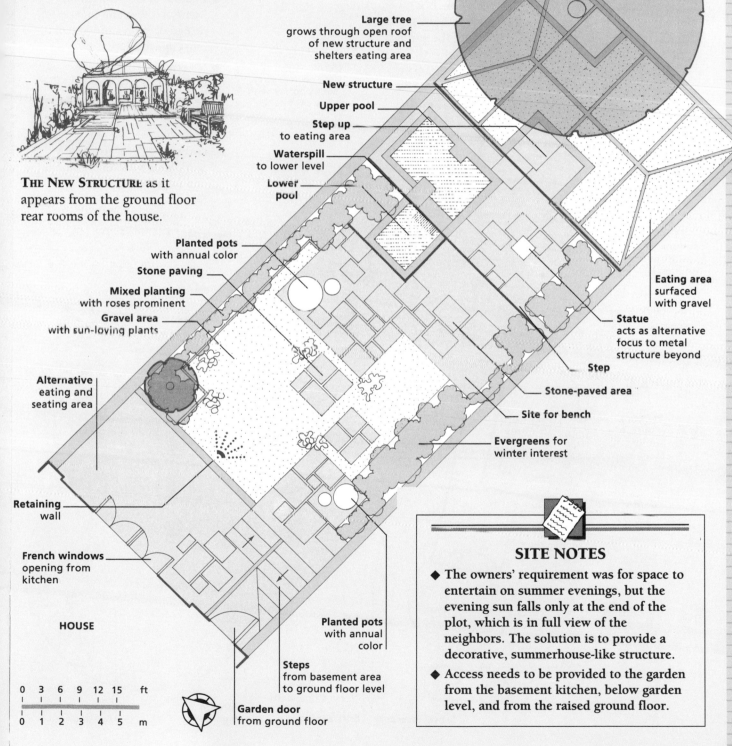

Large tree grows through open roof of new structure and shelters eating area

New structure

Upper pool

Step up to eating area

Waterspill to lower level

Lower pool

Planted pots with annual color

Stone paving

Mixed planting with roses prominent

Gravel area with sun-loving plants

Alternative eating and seating area

Retaining wall

French windows opening from kitchen

HOUSE

Eating area surfaced with gravel

Statue acts as alternative focus to metal structure beyond

Step

Stone-paved area

Site for bench

Evergreens for winter interest

Planted pots with annual color

Steps from basement area to ground floor level

Garden door from ground floor

0 3 6 9 12 15 ft
0 1 2 3 4 5 m

SITE NOTES

◆ The owners' requirement was for space to entertain on summer evenings, but the evening sun falls only at the end of the plot, which is in full view of the neighbors. The solution is to provide a decorative, summerhouse-like structure.

◆ Access needs to be provided to the garden from the basement kitchen, below garden level, and from the raised ground floor.

19 A COUNTRY HOUSE WITH A VIEW

THE HOUSE IS BUILT OF STONE, so the terraces to front and rear are of the same material. Similarly, the gravel used on the forecourt is of the same material as the house. To keep the view into parkland unobscured, a ha-ha (concealed ditch) is used to mark the eastern boundary. The rear is made into a lawn with shrub screens at the sides only.

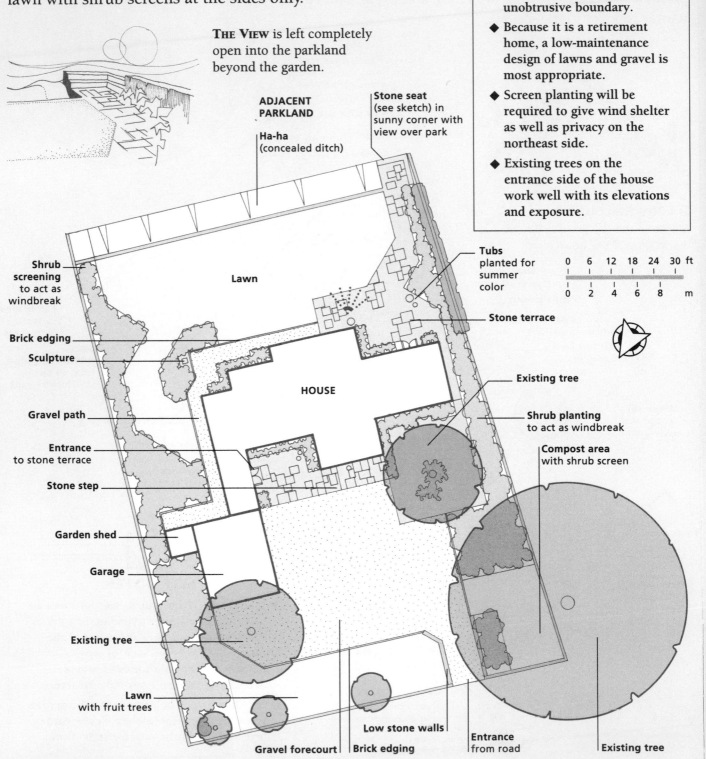

THE VIEW is left completely open into the parkland beyond the garden.

SITE NOTES

◆ This house has fine views over open parkland to the rear. A ha-ha (concealed ditch) would make a suitable, unobtrusive boundary.

◆ Because it is a retirement home, a low-maintenance design of lawns and gravel is most appropriate.

◆ Screen planting will be required to give wind shelter as well as privacy on the northeast side.

◆ Existing trees on the entrance side of the house work well with its elevations and exposure.

ADJACENT PARKLAND

Ha-ha (concealed ditch)

Stone seat (see sketch) in sunny corner with view over park

Lawn

Tubs planted for summer color

0 6 12 18 24 30 ft
0 2 4 6 8 m

Stone terrace

Shrub screening to act as windbreak

Brick edging

Sculpture

Gravel path

Entrance to stone terrace

Stone step

Garden shed

Garage

Existing tree

Lawn with fruit trees

HOUSE

Existing tree

Shrub planting to act as windbreak

Compost area with shrub screen

Low stone walls

Gravel forecourt

Brick edging

Entrance from road

Existing tree

20 AN EASY-CARE TOWN GARDEN

TO MAKE A LARGER AREA of terracing, the lawn is set at an angle; this gives the additional benefit of a hard surface leading from the house to the rear gate without the need to devise a separate path. The pergola helps to create a feeling of being *in* the site rather than on it – it will take three or four years to get sufficient greenery to fill in the garden. A bed of annuals would be an alternative to the pool, making a very strong central statement and holding the eye firmly in the site.

SITE NOTES

◆ This is the owners' first home. It is newly built and the site is barren.

◆ The requirement is for a garden with plenty of space to sunbathe (the garden is sunny) and eat outside, with a minimum of maintenance – the owners are first-time gardeners. Therefore generous terracing and a small lawn seem appropriate.

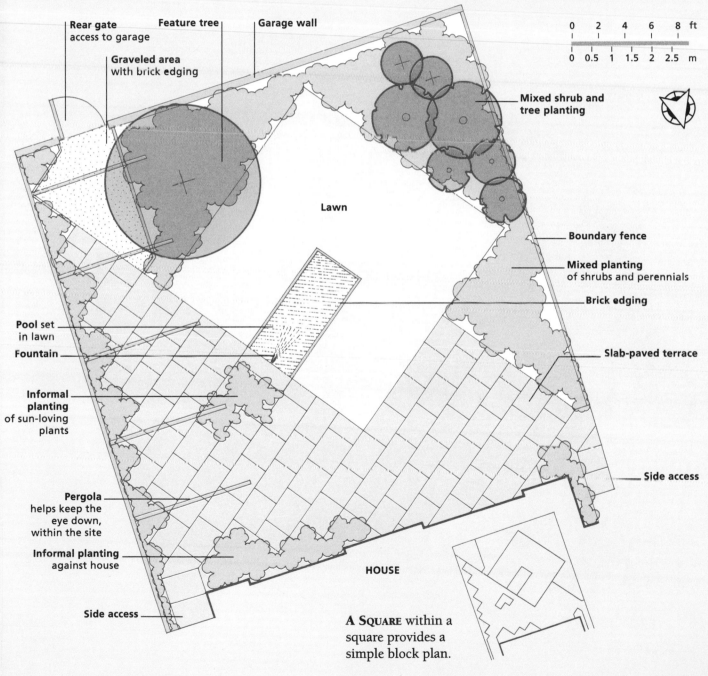

Rear gate
access to garage

Feature tree

Garage wall

Graveled area
with brick edging

Mixed shrub and
tree planting

Lawn

Boundary fence

Mixed planting
of shrubs and perennials

Brick edging

Pool set
in lawn

Fountain

Slab-paved terrace

Informal
planting
of sun-loving
plants

Side access

Pergola
helps keep the
eye down,
within the site

Informal planting
against house

HOUSE

Side access

A SQUARE within a square provides a simple block plan.

21 A COUNTRY HOUSE IN WOODLAND

WITH A GLORIOUS LANDSCAPE as its surrounding, a garden need do no more than set the house in its environs. On the western side, therefore, decking and terracing lead down to lawns that swoop away to the tops of trees on the banks below. Wildflowers are planted in shaped areas of rough grass to the sides of the garden. The patterns of the layout are geometric, like those of the house, but abstracted and extended to blend into the countryside.

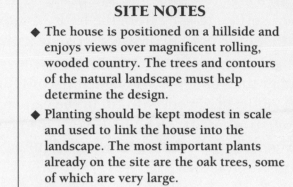

SITE NOTES

◆ The house is positioned on a hillside and enjoys views over magnificent rolling, wooded country. The trees and contours of the natural landscape must help determine the design.

◆ Planting should be kept modest in scale and used to link the house into the landscape. The most important plants already on the site are the oak trees, some of which are very large.

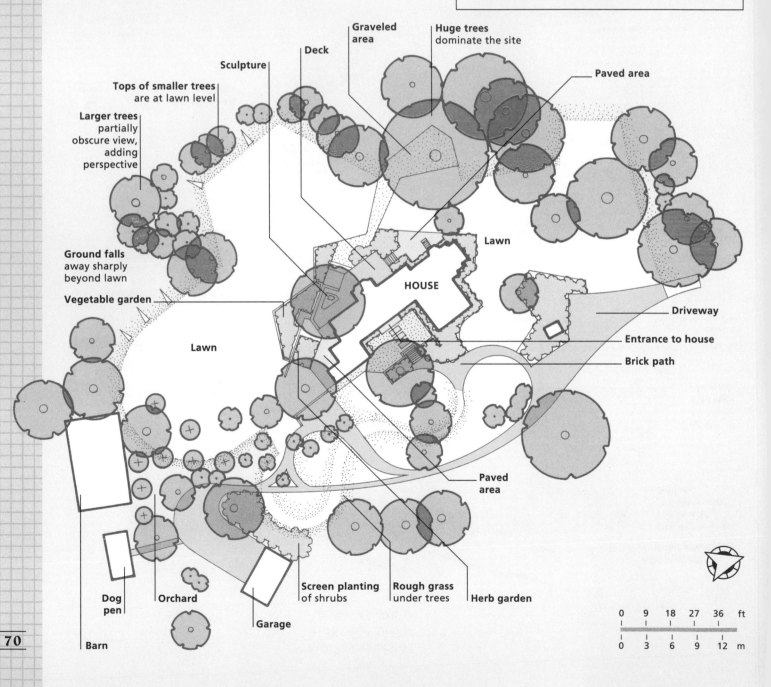

Graveled area

Deck

Sculpture

Huge trees dominate the site

Paved area

Tops of smaller trees are at lawn level

Larger trees partially obscure view, adding perspective

Lawn

HOUSE

Ground falls away sharply beyond lawn

Driveway

Vegetable garden

Entrance to house

Brick path

Lawn

Paved area

Dog pen

Orchard

Screen planting of shrubs

Rough grass under trees

Herb garden

Garage

Barn

| 0 | 9 | 18 | 27 | 36 | ft |
| 0 | 3 | 6 | 9 | 12 | m |

SITE DETAIL

THE TERRACES are designed to work with the rooms they adjoin. The deck, for example, to be used for summer entertaining, is outside the foyer; similarly, the breakfast terrace and herb garden are close to the kitchen. The shapes of the terraces were decreed partly by practicality (the deck should have sun and shade), but also by the need to fit with the contours of the garden.

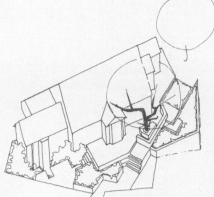

A PROJECTION demonstrates more clearly than a plan could the different levels in a complex design such as this.

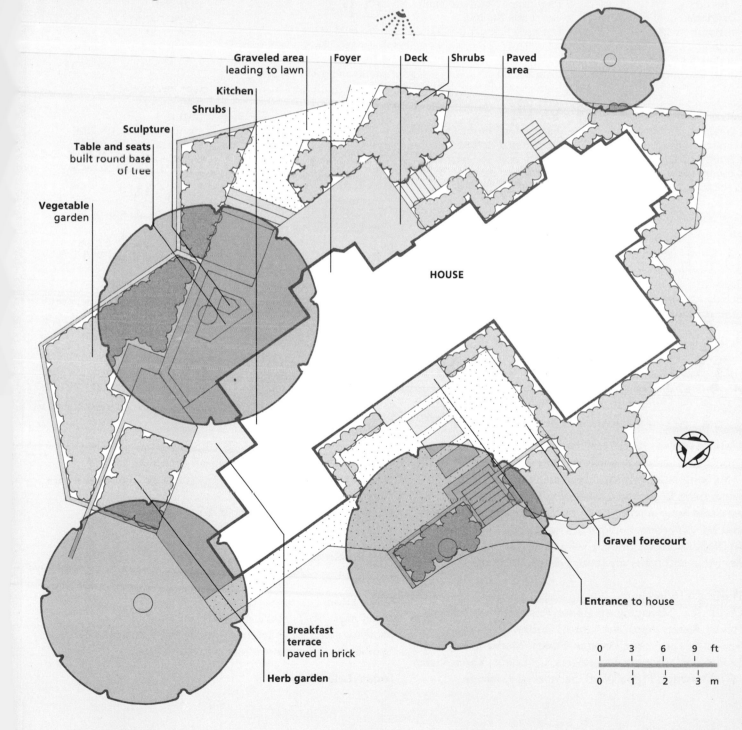

Graveled area leading to lawn
Foyer
Deck
Shrubs
Paved area
Kitchen
Shrubs
Sculpture
Table and seats built round base of tree
Vegetable garden
HOUSE
Gravel forecourt
Entrance to house
Breakfast terrace paved in brick
Herb garden

0	3	6	9	ft
0	1	2	3	m

INDEX

ACKNOWLEDGMENTS

John Brookes:
I would like to credit everyone who helped me in this production – though small, it was complicated.
My long-suffering editor and art editor at Dorling Kindersley, Rosie and Carole. Michael Zinn, my assistant, who acted both as a competent draftsperson and liaison between all parties, and lastly, my secretary, Jill Robertson-Macdonald, who from time to time mops my brow and types my texts. I thank them all.

Dorling Kindersley:
Carole Ash, Managing Art Editor; Rosie Pearson, Managing Editor; Karen Ward, Art Editor; Susannah Marriott, Senior Editor; Lorna Damms, Editor; Maryann Rogers, Production Manager; Ray Rogers, US Editor; Karen Ruane, DTP Designer; Pippa Ward, Secretarial Assistant

Photography:
Studio photography pages 18-29 Ray Gaffney
Location photography pages 30-48 John Brookes
Additional photography Steve Gorton page 39cl, Tim Ridley page 1, Dave King page 5cl
Photographs page 5c, cb, cr, rb Carole Ash
Hand model Kate Scott

Page 7cl Bauhaus-Archiv, Berlin
Page 7tr Pier Gallery, Stromness, Orkney

Illustration:
Plans pages 50-71 Joe Robinson
Working plans and sketches John Brookes and Michael Zinn
Symbols for information boxes Sarah Ponder

Index: Leigh Priest